D1542034

# Selected Titles in This Series

# Codes and Curves

STUDENT MATHEMATICAL LIBRARY
Ω IAS/PARK CITY MATHEMATICAL SUBSERIES
Volume 7

# Codes and Curves

Judy L. Walker

American Mathematical Society
Institute for Advanced Study

2000 *Mathematics Subject Classification.* Primary 11T71, 94B27;
Secondary 11D45, 11G20, 14H50, 94B05, 94B65.

The author was supported in part by NSF grant #DMS 9709388.

---

**Library of Congress Cataloging-in-Publication Data**

Walker, Judy L., 1969–
    Codes and curves / Judy L. Walker.
        p. cm. — (Student mathematical library, ISSN 1520-9121 ; v. 7. IAS/Park
City mathematical subseries)
    Includes bibliographical references.
    ISBN 0-8218-2628-X (softcover : alk. paper)
    1. Coding theory.    2. Curves, Algebraic.    I. Title.    II. Student mathematical
library ; v. 7.    III. Student mathematical library. IAS/Park City mathematical
subseries.
QA268 .W345    2000
003′.54—dc21                                                          00-038112

---

# Contents

# IAS/Park City Mathematics Institute

The IAS/Park City Mathematics Institute (PCMI) was founded in 1991 as part of the "Regional Geometry Institute" initiative of the National Science Foundation. In mid 1993 the program found an institutional home at the Institute for Advanced Study (IAS) in Princeton, New Jersey. The PCMI will continue to hold summer programs alternately in Park City and in Princeton.

The IAS/Park City Mathematics Institute encourages both research and education in mathematics, and fosters interaction between the two. The three-week summer institute offers programs for researchers and postdoctoral scholars, graduate students, undergraduate students, high school teachers, mathematics education researchers, and undergraduate faculty. The summer institute is preceded by the Mentoring Program for Women in Mathematics. One of PCMI's main goals is to make all of the participants aware of the total spectrum of activities that occur in mathematics education and research: we wish to involve professional mathematicians in education and to bring modern concepts in mathematics to the attention of educators. To that end the summer institute features general sessions designed to encourage interaction among the various groups. In-year activities at sites around the country form an integral part of the High School Teacher Program.

Each summer a different topic is chosen as the focus of the Research Program and Graduate Summer School. Activities in the Undergraduate Program, and at the Mentoring Program for Women in Mathematics, deal with this topic as well. Lecture notes from the Graduate Summer School are published each year in the IAS/Park City Mathematics Series. Undergraduate course materials, such as the current volume, are now being published as part of the IAS/Park City Mathematical Subseries in the Student Mathematical Library. We are happy to make available more of the excellent resources which have been developed as part of the PCMI.

At the summer institute late afternoons are devoted to seminars of common interest to all participants. Many deal with current issues in education; others treat mathematical topics at a level which encourages broad participation. The PCMI has also spawned interactions between universities and high schools at a local level. We hope to share these activities with a wider audience in future volumes.

David R. Morrison, Series Editor

February, 2000

# Preface

These notes summarize a series of lectures I gave as part of the IAS/PCMI Mentoring Program for Women in Mathematics, held May 17-27, 1999 at the Institute for Advanced Study in Princeton, NJ with funding from the National Science Foundation. The material included is not original, but the exposition is new. The booklet [**LG**] also contains an introduction to algebraic geometric coding theory, but its intended audience is researchers specializing in either coding theory or algebraic geometry and wanting to understand the connections between the two subjects. These notes, on the other hand, are designed for a general mathematical audience. In fact, the lectures were originally designed for undergraduates.

I have tried to retain the conversational tone of the lectures, and I hope that the reader will find this monograph both accessible and useful. Exercises are scattered throughout, and the reader is strongly encouraged to work through them.

Of the sources listed in the bibliography, it should be pointed out that [**CLO2**], [**Ga**], [**H**], [**L**], [**MS**], [**NZM**] and [**S**] were used most intensively in preparing these notes. In particular:

- Theorem 1.11, which gives some important properties of cyclic codes, can be found in [**MS**].

- The proof given for the Singleton Bound (Theorem 2.1) is from [**S**].
- The proofs given for the Plotkin Bound (Theorem 2.3), the Gilbert-Varshamov Bound (Theorem 2.4), and the asymptotic Plotkin Bound (Theorem 2.7) are from [**L**].
- Exercise 3.6, about finding points on a hyperbola, is taken from [**NZM**].
- The pictures and examples of singularities (as in Exercise 4.4) are from [**H**].
- The proof of the classification of finite fields outlined in the Exercises in Section B.3 is from [**CLO2**].

More generally, the reader is referred to [**L**], [**MS**], and [**S**] for more information on coding theory, [**H**], [**ST**], and [**CLO2**] for more information on algebraic geometry, and [**Ga**] for more background on abstract algebra. In particular, any results included in these notes without proofs are proven in these sources.

I would like to thank all of the people who contributed to the development of this monograph. In particular, special thanks go to: Chuu-Lian Terng and Karen Uhlenbeck, who organize the Mentoring Program and invited me to speak there; Kirstie Venanzi and especially Catherine Jordan, who provide the staff support for the program as well as for IAS/PCMI; Christine Heitsch, who did a great job coordinating problem sessions for my lectures; Graham Leuschke and Mark Walker, who proofread the various drafts of these notes; and, most importantly, the thirteen amazingly bright undergraduate women who participated in the program — Heidi Basler, Lauren Baynes, Juliana Belding, Mariana Campbell, Janae Caspar, Sarah Gruhn, Catherine Holl, Theresa Kim, Sarah Moss, Katarzyna Potocka, Camilla Smith, Michelle Wang, and Lauren Williams.

Judy L. Walker

# Chapter 1

# Introduction to Coding Theory

## 1.1. Overview

Whenever data is transmitted across a channel, errors are likely to occur. It is the goal of coding theory to find efficient ways of encoding the data so that these errors can be detected, or even corrected. Traditionally, the main tools used in coding theory have been those of combinatorics and group theory. In 1977, V. D. Goppa defined algebraic geometric codes [**Go**], thus allowing a wide range of techniques from algebraic geometry to be applied. Goppa's idea has had a great impact on the field. Not long after Goppa's original paper, Tsfasman, Vladut and Zink [**TVZ**] used modular curves to construct a sequence of codes with asymptotically better parameters than any previously known codes. The goal of this course is to introduce you to some of the basics of coding theory, algebraic geometry, and algebraic geometric codes.

Before we write down a rigorous definition of a code, let's look at some examples. Probably the most commonly seen code in day-to-day life is the International Standardized Book Number (ISBN) Code. Every book is assigned an ISBN, and that ISBN is typically displayed on the back cover of the book. For example, the ISBN for *The Theory of Error-Correcting Codes* by MacWilliams and Sloane

([**MS**]) is 0-444-85193-3. The first nine digits 0-444-85193 contain information about the book. The last "3", however, is a check digit which is chosen on the basis of the first nine. In general, the check digit $a_{10}$ for the ISBN $a_1 - a_2 a_3 a_4 - a_5 a_6 a_7 a_8 a_9$ is chosen by computing $a_{10}' := (a_1 + 2a_2 + \cdots + 9a_9)$. If $a_{10}' \equiv i \pmod{11}$ for some $i$ with $0 \leq i \leq 9$, we set $a_{10} = i$. If $a_{10}' \equiv 10 \pmod{11}$, we set $a_{10}$ to be the symbol "$X$". The point is that every book is assigned an ISBN using the same system for choosing a check digit, and so, for example, if you are working in the Library of Congress cataloging new books and you make a mistake when typing in this number, the computer can be programmed to catch your error.

The ISBN Code is a very simple code. It is not hard to see that it *detects* all single-digit errors (a mistake is made in one position) and all transposition errors (the numbers in two positions are flipped). It cannot *correct* any single-digit or transposition errors, but this is not a huge liability, since one can easily just type in the correct ISBN (re-send the message) if a mistake of this type is made. Further, the ISBN code is efficient, since only one non-information symbol needs to be used for every nine-symbol piece of data.

The so-called Repetition Codes provide an entire class of simple codes. Suppose, for example, every possible piece of data has been assigned a four bit string (a string of zeros and ones of length four), and suppose that instead of simply transmitting the data, you transmit each piece of data three times. For instance, the data string 1011 would be transmitted as 1011 1011 1011. If one error occurs, then that error would be contained in one of the three blocks. Thus the other two blocks would still agree, and we would be able to detect and correct the error. If we wanted to be able to correct two errors, we would simply transmit each piece of data five times, and in general, to correct $t$ errors, we would transmit the data $2t + 1$ times.

The Repetition Codes have an advantage over the ISBN Code in that they can actually correct errors rather than solely detect them. However, they are very inefficient, since if we want to be able to correct just one error, we need to transmit a total of three symbols for every information symbol.

We are now in a position to make some definitions.

**Definition 1.1.** A *code* $C$ over an *alphabet* $A$ is simply a subset of $A^n := A \times \cdots \times A$ ($n$ copies).

In this course, $A$ will always be a finite field, but you should be aware that much work has been done recently with codes over finite rings; see Project C.6. Appendix B discusses finite fields, but for now, you may just think of the binary field $\mathbb{F}_2 := \{0, 1\}$, where addition and multiplication are done modulo 2. More generally, for any prime $p$, we have a field $\mathbb{F}_p := \{0, 1, \ldots, p-1\}$ with addition and multiplication modulo $p$.

**Definition 1.2.** Elements of a code are called *codewords*, and the *length* of the code is $n$, where $C \subseteq A^n$. If $A$ is a field, $C$ is called a *linear code* if it is a vector subspace of $A^n$, and in this case the *dimension* $k$ of $C$ is defined to be the dimension of $C$ as a vector space over $A$. Notice that if $A = \mathbb{F}_q$ is the finite field with $q$ elements, and $C$ is a linear code over $A$, then $k = \log_q(\#C)$, where $\#C$ is the number of codewords in $C$. Together with the *minimum distance* $d_{\min}$ of $C$ which we define below, $n$ and $k$ (or $n$ and $\#C$ in the nonlinear case) are called the *parameters* of $C$.

If $C$ is a linear code of length $n$ and dimension $k$ over $A$, we can find $k$ basis elements for $C$, each of which will be a vector of length $n$. We form a $k \times n$ matrix by simply taking the basis elements as the rows, and this matrix is called a *generator matrix* for $C$.

Notice that if $G$ is a generator matrix for $C$, then $C$ is exactly the set $\{\mathbf{u}G \mid \mathbf{u} \in A^k\}$. For example, the matrix

$$\begin{pmatrix} 1 & 1 & 0 \\ 0 & 1 & 1 \end{pmatrix}$$

is a generator matrix for a linear code of length 3 and dimension 2.

**Definition 1.3.** For $\mathbf{x} = (x_1, \ldots, x_n)$, $\mathbf{y} = (y_1, \ldots, y_n) \in A^n$, we define the *Hamming distance* from $\mathbf{x}$ to $\mathbf{y}$ to be

$$d(\mathbf{x}, \mathbf{y}) := \#\{i \mid x_i \neq y_i\}.$$

For $\mathbf{x} \in A^n$, we also define the *Hamming weight* of $\mathbf{x}$ to be $wt(\mathbf{x}) = d(\mathbf{x}, (0, 0, \ldots, 0))$.

**Exercise 1.4.** Show that the Hamming distance in fact defines a metric on $A^n$. In other words, show that for all $\mathbf{x}, \mathbf{y}, \mathbf{z} \in A^n$, we have:

    **a)** $d(\mathbf{x}, \mathbf{y}) \geq 0$, with $d(\mathbf{x}, \mathbf{y}) = 0$ if and only if $\mathbf{x} = \mathbf{y}$,

    **b)** $d(\mathbf{x}, \mathbf{y}) = d(\mathbf{y}, \mathbf{x})$, and

    **c)** $d(\mathbf{x}, \mathbf{y}) + d(\mathbf{y}, \mathbf{z}) \geq d(\mathbf{x}, \mathbf{z})$.

**Definition 1.5.** The *minimum distance* of $C$ is

$$d_{\min} := d_{\min}(C) = \min\{d(\mathbf{x}, \mathbf{y}) \mid \mathbf{x}, \mathbf{y} \in C \text{ and } \mathbf{x} \neq \mathbf{y}\}$$

If the meaning is clear from context, we will often drop the subscript and simply write $d$ for the minimum distance of a code.

**Exercise 1.6.** Show that if $C$ is a linear code then the minimum distance of $C$ is $\min\{wt(\mathbf{x}) \mid \mathbf{x} \in C \text{ and } \mathbf{x} \neq (0, 0, \ldots, 0)\}$. In other words, show that for linear codes, the minimum distance is the same as the *minimum weight*.

Let's now return to our examples. The ISBN Code is a code of length 10 over $\mathbb{F}_{11}$ (where the symbol $X$ stands for the element $10 \in \mathbb{F}_{11}$). It is a nonlinear code since the $X$ can never appear in the first nine positions of the code. It has $10^9$ codewords, and the minimum distance is 2. Our Repetition Code is a linear code over $\mathbb{F}_2$ of length $4r$, where $r$ is the number of times we choose to repeat each piece of data. The dimension is 4, and the minimum distance is $r$.

Why are the dimension (or number of codewords) and minimum distance of a code important? Suppose $C$ is a linear code over an alphabet $A$ which has length $n$, dimension $k$, and minimum distance $d$. We may think of each codeword as having $k$ information symbols and $n - k$ checks. Thus, we want $k$ large with respect to $n$ so that we are not transmitting a lot of extraneous symbols. This makes our code efficient. On the other hand, the value of $d$ determines how many errors our code can correct. To see this, for $\mathbf{x} \in A^n$ and a positive integer $t$, define $B_t(\mathbf{x})$ to be the ball of radius $t$ centered at $\mathbf{x}$. In other words, $B_t(\mathbf{x})$ is the set of all vectors in $A^n$ which are Hamming distance at most $t$ away from $\mathbf{x}$. Since $C$ has minimum distance $d$, two balls of radius $\lfloor \frac{d-1}{2} \rfloor$ centered at distinct codewords cannot intersect. Thus, if at most $\lfloor \frac{d-1}{2} \rfloor$ errors are made in transmission, the received word will lie in a unique ball of radius $\lfloor \frac{d-1}{2} \rfloor$, and that ball will be centered at the correct codeword. In other words, a code of minimum distance $d$ can correct up to $\lfloor \frac{d-1}{2} \rfloor$ errors, so we want $d$ large with respect to $n$ as well.

The question now, of course, is: If we say that a linear code is good if both $k$ and $d$ are large with respect to $n$, then just how good can a code be?

As a partial answer to this question, let's turn now to the Reed-Solomon codes. Let $\mathbb{F}_q$ be the field with $q$ elements. For any non-negative integer $r$, define $L_r := \{f \in \mathbb{F}_q[x] \mid \deg(f) \leq r\} \cup \{0\}$. Note that $L_r$ is a vector space over the field $\mathbb{F}_q$.

**Exercise 1.7.** Show that $\dim_{\mathbb{F}_q}(L_r) = r + 1$ by finding an explicit basis.

**Definition 1.8.** Label the $q - 1$ nonzero elements of $\mathbb{F}_q$ as $\alpha_1, \ldots, \alpha_{q-1}$ and pick $k \in \mathbb{Z}$ with $1 \leq k \leq q - 1$. Then the *Reed-Solomon Code $RS(k, q)$* is defined to be

$$RS(k, q) := \{(f(\alpha_1), \ldots, f(\alpha_{q-1})) \mid f \in L_{k-1}\}.$$

Notice that $RS(k, q)$ is a subset of $\mathbb{F}_q^{q-1} := \mathbb{F}_q \times \cdots \times \mathbb{F}_q$ ($q - 1$ copies), so $RS(k, q)$ is a code over the alphabet $\mathbb{F}_q$. Further, since the map $\epsilon : L_k \to \mathbb{F}_q^{q-1}$ given by $\epsilon(f) = (f(\alpha_1), \ldots, f(\alpha_{q-1}))$ is a linear transformation (see Definition A.21) and $RS(k, q)$ is its image, $RS(k, q)$ is a linear code. What are the parameters of $RS(k, q)$? Certainly the length is $n = q - 1$ and the dimension is at most $\dim L_{k-1} = k$. If $\epsilon(f) = \epsilon(g)$, then $f - g$ has at least $q - 1$ roots, so by Exercise B.10, $f - g$ has degree at least $q - 1$. But $f - g \in L_k$, which implies $f = g$. Thus $C$ has dimension exactly $k$. To find the minimum distance, we'll use Exercise 1.6 and find the minimum weight instead. So, suppose $f \in L_{k-1}$ and $wt(\epsilon(f)) = d = d_{\min}$. Then $f$ has at least $n - d$ zeros, so it has degree at least $n - d$ (again using Exercise B.10). Since $f \in L_{k-1}$, this means that $n - d \leq k - 1$, or, equivalently, $d \geq n - k + 1$.

In Chapter 2.1, we will show that, in fact, we have $d = n - k + 1$.

## 1.2. Cyclic Codes

Before we move on, we should spend a little time on cyclic codes. This class of codes is very important. In particular, some of the codes given as possible project topics in Appendix C are cyclic codes.

**Definition 1.9.** A linear code $C$ is called a *cyclic code* if it has the following property: whenever $(c_0, c_1, \ldots, c_{n-1}) \in C$, it is also true that $(c_1, c_2, \ldots, c_{n-1}, c_0) \in C$.

More generally, the *automorphism group* $\mathrm{Aut}(C)$ of a code $C$ is the set of permutations $\sigma \in S_n$ such that $\sigma(\mathbf{c}) \in C$ for all $\mathbf{c} \in C$, where $\sigma(c_0, \ldots, c_{n-1}) = (c_{\sigma(0)}, \ldots, c_{\sigma(n-1)})$. In other words, the code $C$ is cyclic if and only if the permutation $\sigma = (0, 1, 2, \ldots, n-1)$ is in $\mathrm{Aut}(C)$.

There is a very nice algebraic way of looking at cyclic codes which we will now investigate. Let $C$ be a cyclic code over the field $\mathbb{F}_q$. As in Appendix A, we set $R_n := \mathbb{F}_q[x]/\langle x^n - 1 \rangle$. We can think of elements of $R_n$ as polynomials of degree at most $n-1$ over $\mathbb{F}_q$, where multiplication is done as usual except that $x^n = 1$, $x^{n+1} = x$, and so on (see Exercise A.17). Thus, we can identify $C$ with

$$I_C := \{\mathbf{c}(x) := c_0 + c_1 x + \cdots + c_{n-1}x^{n-1} \in R_n \mid$$
$$\mathbf{c} := (c_0, c_1, \ldots, c_{n-1}) \in C\}.$$

(This is the reason for indexing the coordinates of a cyclic code beginning with 0 rather than 1.)

**Exercise 1.10.** Let $C$ be a cyclic code. Show that $I_C$ is an ideal of $R_n$.

Exercise A.13 shows that every ideal of $\mathbb{F}_q[x]$ is principal, generated by the unique monic polynomial of smallest degree inside the ideal. The next Theorem first shows that the same is true for ideals of $R_n$, then gives some important properties of that polynomial.

**Theorem 1.11.** *Let $I$ be an ideal of $R_n$ and let $g(x) \in I$ be a monic polynomial of minimal degree. Let $\ell = \deg(g(x))$. Then*

**a)** $g(x)$ *is the only monic polynomial of degree $\ell$ in $I$.*

**b)** $g(x)$ *generates $I$ as an ideal of $R_n$.*

**c)** $g(x)$ *divides* $x^n - 1$ *as elements of* $\mathbb{F}_q[x]$.

**d)** *If* $I = I_C$ *for some cyclic code* $C$, *then* $\dim C = n - \ell$.

**Proof.** Suppose first that $f(x) \in I$ is monic of degree $\ell$. If $f(x) \neq g(x)$, then $f(x) - g(x)$ is a polynomial of degree strictly less than $\ell$ in $I$. Multiplying by an appropriate scalar yields a monic polynomial, which contradicts the minimality of $\ell$, proving (a).

To prove (b), let $c(x)$ be any element of $I$. Lifting to $\mathbb{F}_q[x]$, we can use the division algorithm to write $c(x) = f(x)g(x) + r(x)$ for polynomials $f(x)$ and $r(x)$ with $r(x)$ either 0 or of degree strictly less than $\ell$. Since $c(x)$, $g(x)$ and $r(x)$ all have degree less than $n$, it must also be true that $f(x)$ has degree less than $n$, so this equation makes sense in $R_n$ as well. But then we have $r(x) = c(x) - f(x)g(x) \in I$, which means $r(x) = 0$ by minimality of $\ell$.

For (c), use the division algorithm in $\mathbb{F}_q[x]$ to write $x^n - 1 = q(x)g(x) + r(x)$ with $r(x)$ either 0 or having degree strictly less than $\ell$. Passing to $R_n$, we have $r(x) = -q(x)g(x) \in I$, which implies $r(x) = 0$ in $R_n$ by minimality of $\ell$. Thus $r(x) = 0$ in $\mathbb{F}_q[x]$ as well since otherwise $x^n - 1$ divides $r(x)$, which makes $r(x)$ have degree at least $n > \ell$.

Finally, let $\mathbf{c} \in C$ be any codeword. Then $\mathbf{c}(x) \in \langle g(x) \rangle \subset R_n$, so there is some $f(x) \in R_n$ with $\mathbf{c}(x) = f(x)g(x)$. In $\mathbb{F}_q[x]$, then, we have $\mathbf{c}(x) = f(x)g(x) + e(x)(x^n - 1)$ for some polynomial $e(x) \in \mathbb{F}_q[x]$. Using (c), we have $\mathbf{c}(x) = g(x)(f(x) + e(x)q(x))$, where $g(x)q(x) = x^n - 1$. Setting $h(x) = f(x) + e(x)q(x)$, we have $\mathbf{c}(x) = g(x)h(x)$, where $\deg(h(x)) \leq n - \ell - 1$. Thus the codewords of $C$, when thought of as elements of $\mathbb{F}_q[x]$, are precisely the polynomials of the form $g(x)h(x)$, where $h(x) \in L_{n-\ell-1}$, so $\dim C = \dim L_{n-\ell-1} = n - \ell$. This proves (d). $\square$

Because of the importance of this generator of the ideal $I_C$, we give it a special name.

**Definition 1.12.** If $C$ is a cyclic code, we define the *generator polynomial* for $C$ to be the unique monic polynomial $g(x) \in I_C$ of minimal degree.

# Chapter 2

# Bounds on Codes

## 2.1. Bounds

We have already seen that a linear code $C$ of length $n$, dimension $k$ and minimum distance $d$ is efficient if $k$ is large (with respect to $n$) and it corrects many errors if $d$ is large (with respect to $n$). We are thus prompted to ask the question: Given $n$ and $k$, how large can $d$ be? Or, equivalently: Given $n$ and $d$, how large can $k$ be? In this chapter, we will consider three partial answers to these questions.

**Theorem 2.1.** (Singleton Bound) *Let $C$ be a linear code of length $n$, dimension $k$, and minimum distance $d$ over $\mathbb{F}_q$. Then $d \leq n-k+1$.*

This shows that the minimum distance of the Reed-Solomon code $RS(k, q)$ is exactly $n - k + 1$. Any code having parameters which meet the Singleton Bound is called an *MDS code*. (MDS stands for Maximum Distance Separable.)

There are several proofs one can give for this theorem. We will give one which relies only on linear algebra. For others, see [**MS**].

**Proof of Theorem 2.1.** Begin by defining a subset $W \subseteq \mathbb{F}_q^n$ by

$$W := \{\mathbf{a} = (a_1, \ldots, a_n) \in \mathbb{F}_q^n \mid a_d = a_{d+1} = \cdots = a_n = 0\}.$$

For any $\mathbf{a} \in W$, we have $wt(\mathbf{a}) \leq d - 1$, so $W \cap C = \{0\}$. Thus $\dim(W + C) = \dim W + \dim C$, where $W + C$ is the subspace of $\mathbb{F}_q^n$

defined by

$$W + C := \{\mathbf{w} + \mathbf{c} \mid \mathbf{w} \in W \text{ and } \mathbf{c} \in C\}.$$

But $\dim W = d - 1$ and $\dim C = k$, so this says that $d - 1 + k \leq n$, or $d \leq n - k + 1$.                                                    □

Theorem 2.1 shows that if we consider codes of length $q - 1$ and dimension $k$, there are no codes better than the Reed-Solomon codes. However, the Reed-Solomon codes are a very restrictive class of codes because the length is so small with respect to the alphabet size. (Reed-Solomon codes don't even make sense over $\mathbb{F}_2$!) Further, the Main Conjecture on MDS Codes ([**MS**]) essentially asserts that all MDS codes are short. In practice, we want to work with codes which are long with respect to the alphabet size. Thus we look for codes which are long, efficient, and correct many errors, but which perhaps are not optimal with respect to the Singleton Bound.

Although the proof given above works only for linear codes, the Singleton Bound is in fact true for nonlinear codes as well. The statement in this more general case is: If $C$ is a code of length $n$ with $M$ codewords and minimum distance $d$ over an alphabet of size $q$, then $M \leq q^{n-d+1}$.

The following definition will help us state our bounds more clearly.

**Definition 2.2.** Let $q$ be a prime power and let $n$, $d$ be positive integers with $d \leq n$. Then the quantity $A_q(n, d)$ is defined as the maximum value of $M$ such that there is a code over $\mathbb{F}_q$ of length $n$ with $M$ codewords and minimum distance $d$.

By the Singleton Bound, we immediately have that $A_q(n, d) \leq q^{n-d+1}$, but the Main Conjecture claims that this bound is not sharp for long codes. We now give both an upper bound which works for long codes and a lower bound on $A_q(n, d)$.

**Theorem 2.3.** (Plotkin Bound) *Set* $\theta = 1 - 1/q$. *Then* $A_q(n, d) = 0$ *if* $d < \theta n$ *and*

$$A_q(n, d) \leq \frac{d}{d - \theta n} \qquad \text{if } d > \theta n.$$

**Proof.** Let $C$ be a code of length $n$ with $M$ codewords and minimum distance $d$ over the field $\mathbb{F}_q$. Set $S = \sum d(\mathbf{x}, \mathbf{y})$, where the sum runs over all ordered pairs of distinct codewords in $C$. Since the distance between any two codewords is at least $d$, and there are $M(M-1)$ possible ordered pairs of distinct codewords, we immediately have $S \geq M(M-1)d$.

Now we'll derive an upper bound on $S$. Form an $M \times n$ matrix where the rows are the codewords of $C$. Consider any one column of this matrix, and let $m_\alpha$ be the number of times the element $\alpha$ of $\mathbb{F}_q$ occurs in this column. (Note that $\sum m_\alpha = M$.) Then $M - m_\alpha$ codewords have some other entry in that column and there are $n$ columns total, so assuming this column is the one in which codewords differ the most, we have

$$S \leq n \sum_{\alpha \in \mathbb{F}_q} m_\alpha (M - m_\alpha)$$

$$= nM \sum_{\alpha \in \mathbb{F}_q} m_\alpha - n \sum_{\alpha \in \mathbb{F}_q} m_\alpha^2$$

$$= n(M^2 - \sum_{\alpha \in \mathbb{F}_q} m_\alpha^2).$$

Now recall the Cauchy-Schwarz inequality: If $\mathbf{a} = (a_1, \ldots, a_r)$ and $\mathbf{b} = (b_1, \ldots, b_r)$ are vectors of length $r$, set $\mathbf{a} \cdot \mathbf{b} := \sum a_i b_i$, and $||\mathbf{a}|| := (\sum a_i^2)^{1/2}$. Then $||\mathbf{a} \cdot \mathbf{b}|| \leq ||\mathbf{a}|| \, ||\mathbf{b}||$. So setting $\mathbf{a} = (m_\alpha)_{\alpha \in \mathbb{F}_q}$ and $\mathbf{b} = (1, \ldots, 1)$, we get

$$\sum_{\alpha \in \mathbb{F}_q} m_\alpha \leq \left( \sum_{\alpha \in \mathbb{F}_q} m_\alpha^2 \right)^{\frac{1}{2}} \sqrt{q}.$$

Squaring both sides and dividing through by $q$ yields

$$\frac{1}{q} \left( \sum_{\alpha \in \mathbb{F}_q} m_\alpha \right)^2 \leq \sum_{\alpha \in \mathbb{F}_q} m_\alpha^2.$$

Substituting, we get $S \leq n(M^2 - M^2/q) = nM^2\theta$, where $\theta = 1 - 1/q$. Putting this all together, we have

$$dM(M-1) \leq S \leq nM^2\theta.$$

This can be rewritten as $M \leq d/(d - \theta n)$, giving the statement of the theorem.                                                                                 □

Before we can state our lower bound on $A_q(n, d)$, we must review some notation. Recall that for any $\mathbf{x} \in \mathbb{F}_q^n$ and any positive integer $r$, $B_r(\mathbf{x})$ is the ball of radius $r$ centered at $\mathbf{x}$. Note that $\#B_r(\mathbf{x})$ is independent of $\mathbf{x}$ and depends only on $r$, $q$, and $n$. Thus we may let $V_q(n, r)$ denote the number of elements in $B_r(\mathbf{x})$ for any $\mathbf{x} \in \mathbb{F}_q^n$. For any $\mathbf{y} \in B_r(\mathbf{x})$, there are $(q - 1)$ possible values for each of the $r$ positions in which $\mathbf{x}$ and $\mathbf{y}$ differ, so we see that

$$V_q(n, r) := \#B_r(\mathbf{x}) = \sum_{i=0}^{r} \binom{n}{i} (q - 1)^i.$$

We're now ready to state our lower bound:

**Theorem 2.4.** (Gilbert-Varshamov Bound) *The quantity $A_q(n, d)$ satisfies*

$$A_q(n, d) \geq q^n / V_q(n, d - 1).$$

**Proof.** Let $C$ be a (possibly nonlinear) code of length $n$ over $\mathbb{F}_q$ with minimum distance $d$ and $M = A_q(n, d)$ codewords. Let $\mathbf{y} \in \mathbb{F}_q^n$ be arbitrary. If $\mathbf{y}$ doesn't lie in $B_{d-1}(\mathbf{x})$ for any $\mathbf{x} \in C$, then $d(\mathbf{x}, \mathbf{y}) \geq d$ for every $\mathbf{x} \in C$. Thus $C \cup \{\mathbf{y}\}$ is a code of length $n$ with minimum distance $d$ and $M + 1 > A_q(n, d)$ codewords, which is impossible. Thus $\mathbf{y} \in B_{d-1}(\mathbf{x})$ for some $\mathbf{x} \in C$. Therefore the union over all $M$ codewords $\mathbf{x} \in C$ of $B_{d-1}(\mathbf{x})$ must be all of $\mathbb{F}_q^n$, so we have

$$q^n = \#\mathbb{F}_q^n \leq M \cdot V_q(n, d - 1).$$

Rewriting this inequality gives the desired bound.                                 □

## 2.2. Asymptotic Bounds

Since we are looking for codes which have large dimension (or many codewords in the nonlinear case) and large minimum distance with respect to $n$, it makes sense to normalize these parameters by dividing through by $n$. In this spirit, we have:

**Definition 2.5.** Let $C$ be a code over $\mathbb{F}_q$ of length $n$ with $q^k$ codewords and minimum distance $d$. (Note that if $C$ is not linear then $k$

might not be an integer.) The *information rate* of $C$ is $R := k/n$ and the *relative minimum distance* of $C$ is $\delta := d/n$.

Of course, both $R$ and $\delta$ are between 0 and 1, and $C$ is a good code if both $R$ and $\delta$ are close to 1.

Our question of the last section now becomes: Given $\delta$, how large can $R$ be? Building on our previous results, we make the following definition:

**Definition 2.6.** Let $q$ be a prime power and $\delta \in \mathbb{R}$ with $0 \le \delta \le 1$. Then

$$\alpha_q(\delta) := \limsup_{n \to \infty} \frac{1}{n} \log_q A_q(n, \delta n)$$

After some thought, one sees that $\alpha_q(\delta)$ is the largest $R$ such that there is a sequence of codes over $\mathbb{F}_q$ with relative minimum distance converging to $\delta$ and information rate converging to $R$. We will now develop asymptotic versions of the Plotkin and Gilbert-Varshamov bounds, thus giving bounds on the value of $\alpha_q(\delta)$.

**Theorem 2.7.** (Asymptotic Plotkin Bound) *With $\theta = 1 - 1/q$, we have*

$$\begin{aligned}
\alpha_q(\delta) &\le 1 - \delta/\theta, && \text{if } 0 \le \delta \le \theta \\
\alpha_q(\delta) &= 0, && \text{if } \theta \le \delta \le 1
\end{aligned}$$

**Proof.** Let $C$ be a code of length $n$ with $M$ codewords and minimum distance $d$ over $\mathbb{F}_q$. We can "shorten" $C$ by considering the subset of $C$ which ends in a certain symbol and then deleting that symbol. This procedure certainly preserves minimum distance, so if we do it $r$ times, we are left with a code $C'$ with length $n - r$, minimum distance $d$, and at least $M/q^r$ codewords.

Set $n' := \lfloor \frac{d-1}{\theta} \rfloor$ and shorten $C$ a total of $r = n - n'$ times to obtain a code of length $n'$ with $M' \ge M/q^{n-n'}$ codewords. The original Plotkin Bound of Theorem 2.3 gives us

$$\frac{M}{q^{n-n'}} \le M' \le \frac{d}{d - \theta n'} \le d,$$

which immediately gives $M \leq dq^{n-n'}$. Plugging into the definition for $\alpha_q(\delta)$, we have

$$\begin{aligned}
\alpha_q(\delta) &\leq \limsup_{n \to \infty} \frac{1}{n} \log_q(\delta n q^{n-n'}) \\
&= \limsup_{n \to \infty} \left( \frac{\log_q \delta}{n} + \frac{\log_q n}{n} + 1 - \frac{n'}{n} \right) \\
&= 1 - \lim_{n \to \infty} \frac{n'}{n} \\
&= 1 - \delta/\theta.
\end{aligned}$$

The equation

$$\lim_{n \to \infty} n'/n = \lim_{n \to \infty} \left( \frac{d-1}{\theta} \right)/n = \delta/\theta.$$

gives the last step.                                                        $\square$

In order to prove an asymptotic version of the Gilbert-Varshamov Bound, we will need a definition and a lemma. As usual, set $\theta = 1 - 1/q$, and define a function $H_q(x)$ on the interval $0 \leq x \leq \theta$ by

$$H_q(x) := \begin{cases} 0, & x = 0 \\ x \log_q(q-1) - x \log_q x - (1-x) \log_q(1-x), & 0 < x \leq \theta \end{cases}$$

The function $H_q$ is called the *Hilbert entropy function.*

Recall that $V_q(n, r)$ is the number of vectors in any ball of radius $r$ in $\mathbb{F}_q^n$.

**Lemma 2.8.** *For any $\lambda$ with $0 \leq \lambda \leq \theta$, we have*

$$\lim_{n \to \infty} \frac{1}{n} \log_q V_q(n, \lfloor \lambda n \rfloor) = H_q(\lambda).$$

We omit the proof of this lemma. However, it is not difficult and relies on a combinatorial result called Stirling's formula.

**Theorem 2.9.** (Asymptotic Gilbert-Varshamov Bound) *For any $\delta$ with $0 \leq \delta \leq \theta$, we have*

$$\alpha_q(\delta) \geq 1 - H_q(\delta).$$

**Proof.** Simply plug into the definition of $\alpha_q(\delta)$:

$$\alpha_q(\delta) = \limsup_{n \to \infty} \frac{1}{n} \log_q A(n, \delta n)$$

$$\geq \limsup_{n \to \infty} \frac{1}{n} \log_q (q^n / V_q(n, d-1))$$

$$= \lim_{n \to \infty} 1 - \frac{1}{n} \log_q V_q(n, \delta n) = 1 - H_q(\delta),$$

which is what we needed to show. $\square$

Therefore, the possible values for $\alpha_q(\delta)$ lie in the region above the Gilbert-Varshamov curve $R = 1 - H_q(\delta)$ and below the Plotkin line $R = 1 - \delta/\theta$ in the $R$-$\delta$ plane, as indicated by the shaded region in the following picture:

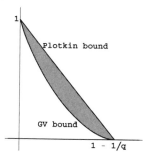

We close this chapter with a bit of history to put things into perspective. There are several known upper bounds on $\alpha_q(\delta)$. The Plotkin bound is not the best one, but we chose to include it because it gives a flavor for the area and because it is simple to prove. On the other hand, the seemingly obvious Gilbert-Varshamov bound was the best known lower bound on $\alpha_q(\delta)$ for a full 30 years following its original discovery in 1952. The existence of a sequence of codes having parameters asymptotically better than those guaranteed by the Gilbert-Varshamov bound was first proven in 1982 by Tsfasman, Vladut, and Zink. Their sequence used algebraic geometry codes, which were introduced by V. D. Goppa in 1977. Our goal for the rest of the course is to develop some algebraic geometry so that we can understand Goppa's construction and see how Tsfasman, Vladut, and Zink came up with their ground-breaking sequence of codes.

# Chapter 3

# Algebraic Curves

## 3.1. Algebraically Closed Fields

We begin this section with a definition:

**Definition 3.1.** A field $k$ is *algebraically closed* if every polynomial in $k[x]$ has at least one root.

For example, $\mathbb{F}_2$ is not algebraically closed since $x^2 + x + 1$ is irreducible over $\mathbb{F}_2$. Similarly, $\mathbb{Q}$ and $\mathbb{R}$ are not algebraically closed since $x^2 + 1$ is irreducible over these fields. However, $\mathbb{C}$ is algebraically closed; this is the Fundamental Theorem of Algebra.

**Exercise 3.2.** Let $\mathbb{F}$ be a finite field. Prove that $\mathbb{F}$ cannot be algebraically closed. Hint: Mimic Euclid's proof that there are infinitely many primes.

Given a field $k$, it is often convenient to look at an algebraically closed field which contains $k$.

**Definition 3.3.** Let $k$ be a field. An *algebraic closure* of $k$ is a field $K$ with $k \subseteq K$ satisfying

- $K$ is algebraically closed, and
- If $L$ is a field such that $k \subseteq L \subseteq K$ and $L$ is algebraically closed, then $L = K$.

In other words, an algebraic closure of $k$ is a "smallest" algebraically closed field containing $k$. There is the following theorem:

**Theorem 3.4.** *Every field has an unique algebraic closure, up to isomorphism.*

Because of this theorem, we can talk of *the* algebraic closure of the field $k$, and we write $\bar{k}$ for this field. For example, $\bar{\mathbb{R}} = \mathbb{C}$. On the other hand, it is known that $\pi$, for example, is not the root of any polynomial over $\mathbb{Q}$, so $\bar{\mathbb{Q}} \subset \mathbb{C}$ but $\bar{\mathbb{Q}} \neq \mathbb{C}$. Also, $\bar{\mathbb{F}}_4 = \bar{\mathbb{F}}_2$, and in general, $\bar{\mathbb{F}}_{p^n} = \bar{\mathbb{F}}_p$.

The following theorem gives a crucial property of algebraically closed fields.

**Theorem 3.5.** *Let $k$ be an algebraically closed field and let $f(x) \in k[x]$ be a polynomial of degree $n$. Then there exists $u \in k^\times := k \setminus \{0\}$ and $\alpha_1, \ldots \alpha_n \in k$ (not necessarily distinct) such that $f(x) = u(x - \alpha_1) \ldots (x - \alpha_n)$. In particular, counting multiplicity, $f$ has exactly $n$ roots in $k$.*

**Proof.** Induct on $n$. If $n = 0$, then $f$ is constant, so $f \in k^\times$. Assume now that every polynomial of degree $n$ can be written in the form of the theorem, and let $f(x) \in k[x]$ have degree $n + 1$. Then since $k$ is algebraically closed, $f$ has a root $\alpha$. Now by Exercise B.10, $f(x) = (x - \alpha)g(x)$ for some $g(x) \in k[x]$ of degree $n$. By the induction hypothesis, we can write $g(x)$ in the desired form, thus giving an appropriate expression for $f(x)$.                                    $\square$

## 3.2. Curves and the Projective Plane

Given a polynomial with integer or rational coefficients (a *Diophantine Equation*), it is a fundamental problem in number theory to find solutions of this equation in either the integers, the positive integers, or the rationals. For example, Fermat's Last Theorem (recently proven by Andrew Wiles) states that there is no solution $(x, y, z)$ in positive integers to the equation $x^n + y^n = z^n$ when $n \geq 3$. The problem of finding positive integers $a, b, c$ which could be the sides of a right triangle (*Pythagorean triples*) could be stated as finding positive integer solutions to the equation $a^2 + b^2 = c^2$. It is often useful to approach these problems by thinking of the equations geometrically and/or modulo some prime $p$. If $f(x,y) = 0$ is a polynomial in two variables, then the equation $f(x,y) = 0$ defines a curve $C_f$ in the plane. This leads us to the study of algebraic curves and algebraic curves over finite fields. The set of solutions to the equation $f(x,y) = 0$ in the field $k$ is denoted $C_f(k)$.

**Exercise 3.6.** The purpose of this problem is to find all rational solutions to the equation $x^2 - 2y^2 = 1$. We will do this graphically, by considering the hyperbola $C_f$ in $\mathbb{R}^2$ defined by the polynomial $f(x,y) = x^2 - 2y^2 - 1$.

    **a)** Show that $(1,0)$ is a point on the hyperbola. Are there any other points with $y$-coordinate 0?

    **b)** Let $L$ be a line with rational slope $t$ which passes through the point $(1,0)$. Write down an equation for the line $L$ in the form $y = p(x)$.

    **c)** Show that the equation $f(x, p(x))$ has exactly 2 solutions $(x,y)$, one of which is $(1,0)$, and the other of which is a rational solution to the equation $x^2 - 2y^2 = 1$.

    **d)** Write down polynomial equations $x = x(t)$, $y = y(t)$ which define infinitely many rational solutions to the equation $x^2 - 2y^2 = 1$.

    **e)** Show that your equations actually give all but two rational solutions to the equation. Which two are missing?

    If we want simultaneous solutions to two polynomial equations in two variables, then we're looking at the intersection of two curves. Let's examine a specific case. Take $f(x,y) = y - x^2$ and $g(x,y) = y - c$ for various choices of $c$. If we take $k = \mathbb{R}$, we can graph these two equations and look for points of intersection. We see that sometimes we have exactly 2 points of intersection. This occurs, for example, if $c = 4$. If $c = 0$, we get only one point, and if $c < 0$, we don't get any at all! However, if we point out that when $c = 0$, the curves are actually tangent at the point of intersection, we can count that as a single point of multiplicity 2. Further, if we extend to $\bar{k} = \mathbb{C}$, we see that we get exactly 2 points of intersection for $c < 0$ as well. More generally, if we take lines of the form $y = mx + b$, we will get either 2,

1, or 0 points of intersection over $\mathbb{R}$ and the situation is as before: If there is one point of intersection, then the line is actually a tangent line. If there are no points of intersection, then we find two when we look in $\mathbb{C}$. It's beginning to look as if $C_f$ and $C_g$ will always intersect in exactly two points, at least if we're willing to count multiplicity and extend to the algebraic closure.

But now replace our $g$ with the vertical line defined by $g(x, y) = x - c$. Regardless of what value of $c$ we choose, there is only one point of intersection and the line is not tangent at that point. Extending to $\mathbb{C}$ doesn't help things at all. But somehow we feel that if we count correctly, there should be two points of intersection between any line and the curve $C_f$, where $f(x, y) = y - x^2$.

Heuristically, the idea is as follows: The curves $x = c$ and $y = x^2$ intersect once "at infinity" as well. In general, a curve $C_f$ where $f(x, y) \in k[x, y]$ is called an *affine* curve. We want to look at the *projective closure* $\widehat{C_f}$ of $C_f$, which amounts to "adding points at infinity". To do this, start by constructing the polynomial $F(X, Y, Z) = Z^d f(X/Z, Y/Z) \in k[X, Y, Z]$, where $d = \deg(f)$.

For example, the curve defined by the polynomial equation $y^2 = x^3 + x + 1$ is $C_f$, where $f(x, y) = y^2 - x^3 - x - 1$. Then $F(X, Y, Z) = Z^3((Y/Z)^2 - (X/Z)^3 - (X/Z) - 1) = Y^2 Z - X^3 - XZ^2 - Z^3$. Notice that every monomial appearing in $F$ has degree exactly $3 = \deg(f)$, and that the task of constructing $F$ amounted to capitalizing and adding enough $Z$'s so that every term would have degree 3. The polynomial $F$ is called the *homogenization* of $f$.

We now ask: How do the solutions $(x_0, y_0)$ to $f(x, y) = 0$ and the solutions $(X_0, Y_0, Z_0)$ to $F(X, Y, Z) = 0$ compare? Three observations are immediate:

- $f(x_0, y_0) = 0 \iff F(x_0, y_0, 1) = 0$
- For any $\alpha \in k^\times$, we have

$$F(\alpha X, \alpha Y, \alpha Z) = (\alpha Z)^d f(\alpha X/\alpha Z, \alpha Y/\alpha Z)$$
$$= \alpha^d F(X, Y, Z),$$

so $F(X_0, Y_0, Z_0) = 0 \iff F(\alpha X_0, \alpha Y_0, \alpha Z_0) = 0$ for all $\alpha \in k^\times$.

- Since $F$ is homogeneous, $F(0,0,0) = 0$.

Because of the third observation, we want to ignore the solution $(0,0,0)$ of $F = 0$. Because of the second, we want to identify the solutions $(X_0, Y_0, Z_0)$ and $(\alpha X_0, \alpha Y_0, \alpha Z_0)$. This leads us to the following definition:

**Definition 3.7.** Let $k$ be a field. The *projective plane* $\mathbb{P}^2(k)$ is defined as
$$\mathbb{P}^2(k) := (k^3 \setminus \{(0,0,0)\})/\sim,$$
where $(X_0, Y_0, Z_0) \sim (X_1, Y_1, Z_1)$ if and only if there is some $\alpha \in k^\times$ with $X_1 = \alpha X_0$, $Y_1 = \alpha Y_0$, and $Z_1 = \alpha Z_0$.

To remind ourselves that points of $\mathbb{P}^2(k)$ are equivalence classes, we write $(X_0 : Y_0 : Z_0)$ for the equivalence class of $(X_0, Y_0, Z_0)$ in $\mathbb{P}^2(k)$.

**Definition 3.8.** Let $k$ be a field, $f(x, y) \in k[x, y]$ a polynomial of degree $d$, and $C_f$ the curve associated to $f$. The *projective closure* of the curve $C_f$ is $\widehat{C_f} := \{(X_0 : Y_0 : Z_0) \in \mathbb{P}^2 \mid F(X_0, Y_0, Z_0) = 0\}$, where $F(X, Y, Z) := Z^d f(X/Z, Y/Z) \in k[X, Y, Z]$ is the *homogenization* of $f$.

By multiplying through by a unit, we can assume the right-most nonzero coordinate of a point of $\mathbb{P}^2(k)$ is 1, so we have
$$\mathbb{P}^2(k) = \{(X_0 : Y_0 : 1) \mid X_0, Y_0 \in k\} \cup$$
$$\{(X_0 : 1 : 0) \mid X_0 \in k\} \cup$$
$$\{(1 : 0 : 0)\}.$$
Any point $(X_0 : Y_0 : Z_0)$ with $Z_0 = 0$ is called a *point at infinity*. Every other point is called *affine*.

**Exercise 3.9.** Suppose $f(x, y) \in k[x, y]$ and $F(X, Y, Z)$ is the homogenization of $f$. Show that $f(x, y) = F(x, y, 1)$.

**Exercise 3.10.** Consider the projective plane $\mathbb{P}^2(\mathbb{R})$.

a) Prove that in $\mathbb{P}^2(\mathbb{R})$, there is a one-to-one correspondence between points at infinity and lines through the origin in $\mathbb{R}^2$.

b) Given a line in $\mathbb{R}^2$ which does not pass through the origin, which point at infinity lies on the projective closure of that line?

Let's return now to our example and see what happens if we consider the intersection in $\mathbb{P}^2$. We have $f(x,y) = y - x^2$, so $F(X,Y,Z) = YZ - X^2$. Also, $g(x,y) = x - c$, so $G(X,Y,Z) = X - cZ$. To find our affine points of intersection, we set $Z = 1$ and find that $Y - X^2 = 0$ and $X = c$. Thus $Y = c^2$ and our only affine point of intersection is $(c : c^2 : 1)$. Now look at points at infinity: $F(X,Y,0) = -X^2$, which is 0 if and only if $X = 0$, so we get the point $(0 : 1 : 0)$ on $\widehat{C_f}$. Since $G(X,Y,0) = X$, this point is certainly on $\widehat{C_g}$ as well. Therefore, we see that if we look in $\mathbb{P}^2$, we get exactly two points of intersection of $\widehat{C_f}$ and $\widehat{C_g}$.

In fact, there is the following theorem:

**Theorem 3.11.** (Bezout's Theorem) *If $f, g \in k[x,y]$ are polynomials of degrees $d$ and $e$ respectively, then $C_f$ and $C_g$ intersect in at most $de$ points. Further, $\widehat{C_f}$ and $\widehat{C_g}$ intersect in exactly $de$ points of $\mathbb{P}^2(\bar{k})$, when points are counted with multiplicity.*

For example, Bezout's theorem says that any two curves defined by quadratic polynomials intersect in exactly four points when counted appropriately. If we set $f_1(x,y) = y - x^2$ and $f_2(x,y) = (y-2)^2 - (x+2)$, then we can graph the curves $C_{f_1}$ and $C_{f_2}$ to find exactly four points of intersection in $\mathbb{R}^2$. However, if we replace $f_2$ with $f_3 = y^2 - (x+2)$, then $C_{f_1}$ and $C_{f_3}$ intersect in only two points in $\mathbb{R}^2$. Allowing complex coordinates, we find the other two points of intersection. On the other hand, even in complex coordinates, the curves $C_{f_1}$ and $C_{f_4}$, where $f_4(x,y) = y + x^2 - 2$, intersect at only two points. If we homogenize, however, we see that $\widehat{C_{f_1}}$ and $\widehat{C_{f_4}}$ intersect at the point $(0 : 1 : 0)$. By Bezout's Theorem, the curves must intersect with multiplicity 2 there. In other words, the curves are tangent at the point $(0 : 1 : 0)$.

**Exercise 3.12.** Let $f(x,y) = x^3 + x^2y - 3xy^2 - 3y^3 + 2x^2 - x + 5$. Find all (complex) points at infinity on $\widehat{C_f}$, the projective closure of $C_f$.

**Exercise 3.13.** Find $C(\mathbb{F}_7)$ where $C$ is the projective closure of the curve defined by the equation $y^2 = x^3 + x + 1$.

# Chapter 4

# Nonsingularity and the Genus

## 4.1. Nonsingularity

For coding theory, one only wants to work with "nice" curves. Since we've already decided to restrict ourselves to plane curves, the only other restriction we will need is that our curves will be *nonsingular*, a notion which we will define below. As nonsingularity and differentiability are closely related, we must first figure out what it means to differentiate over an arbitrary field $k$.

Let $k$ be a field and let $f(x, y) \in k[x, y]$ be a polynomial. If $k = \mathbb{R}$ or $\mathbb{C}$, we understand completely what the partial derivative $f_x$ of $f$ with respect to $x$ is. If $k$ is a field of characteristic $p > 0$ (see Definition B.1), the usual limit definition no longer makes sense. However, for $f(x, y) \in \mathbb{F}_q[x, y]$, we can define the *formal partial derivative* $f_x(x, y) \in k[x, y]$ of $f$ with respect to $x$ by simply declaring that the familiar rules for differentiation are in fact the definition. For example, if $f(x, y) = x^2 + y^3 + xy$, then $f_x(x, y) = 2x + y$ and $f_y(x, y) = 3y^2 + x$ over any field $k$. In particular, if $k = \mathbb{F}_2$, then $f_x(x, y) = y$ and $f_y(x, y) = y^2 + x$. On the other hand, if $k = \mathbb{F}_3$, then $f_x(x, y) = 2x + y$ and $f_y(x, y) = x$.

**Definition 4.1.** Let $k$ be a field and $f(x,y) \in k[x,y]$. A *singular point* of $C_f$ is a point $(x_0, y_0) \in \bar{k} \times \bar{k}$ such that $f(x_0, y_0) = 0$ and $f_x(x_0, y_0) = 0$ and $f_y(x_0, y_0) = 0$. The curve $C_f$ is *nonsingular* if it has no singular points. If $F(X, Y, Z)$ is the homogenization of $f(x, y)$, then $(X_0 : Y_0 : Z_0) \in \mathbb{P}^2(\bar{k})$ is a singular point of $\widehat{C_f}$ if the point is on the curve and all partial derivatives vanish there, i.e., if

$$
\begin{aligned}
F(X_0, Y_0, Z_0) &= F_X(X_0, Y_0, Z_0) \\
&= F_Y(X_0, Y_0, Z_0) \\
&= F_Z(X_0, Y_0, Z_0) \\
&= 0.
\end{aligned}
$$

The curve $\widehat{C_f}$ is *nonsingular* if it has no singular points.

**Exercise 4.2.** Let $f(x, y) \in \mathbb{R}[x, y]$ and suppose $(0, 0)$ is a nonsingular point on $C_f$. If $f_y(0,0) \neq 0$, show that the line $y = mx$, where $m = f_x(0,0)/f_y(0,0)$, is the tangent line to $C_f$ at $(0, 0)$. If $f_y(0, 0) = 0$, show that the line $x = 0$ is the tangent line to $C_f$ at $(0, 0)$.

In general, if $P$ is a nonsingular point on $C_f$, then the line through $P$ with slope $f_x(P)/f_y(P)$ is the tangent line to $C_f$ at $P$. If $f_y(P) = 0$, the tangent line is the vertical line through $P$. Exercise 4.2 proves this (after a change of coordinates).

**Exercise 4.3.** If Definition 4.1 is to make sense, one would expect that if $C_f$ is nonsingular then the only possible singular points of $\widehat{C_f}$ are at infinity. This is true, and follows from the definition of the homogenization of $f$ and the chain rule for partial derivatives. Check it for yourself.

Intuitively, a singular point is a point where the curve doesn't have a well-defined tangent line, or where it intersects itself. Here are four examples of curves (over $\mathbb{R}$) with singularities:

| TACHNODE | NODE | CUSP | TRIPLEPOINT |
|---|---|---|---|
|  | 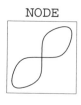 | 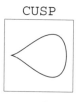 |  |

As an example, let's consider the curve $\widehat{C_f}$, where $f(x, y) = -x^3 + y^2 + x^4 + y^4$ over $\mathbb{C}$. We have $f_x(x, y) = -3x^2 + 4x^3 = x^2(-3 + 4x)$ and $f_y(x, y) = 2y + 4y^3 = 2y(1 + 4y^2)$. In order for $(x_0, y_0)$ to be a singular point, we would need $x_0 = 0$ or $3/4$ and $y_0 = 0$, $\frac{1}{2}i$, or $-\frac{1}{2}i$. A quick check shows that of the 6 possible pairs $(x_0, y_0)$ only $(0, 0)$ is on the curve, so $(0, 0)$ is the only affine singularity. The homogenization of $f$ is $F(X, Y, Z) = -X^3Z + Y^2Z^2 + X^4 + Y^4$, so we have $F_X = -3X^2Z + 4X^3$, $F_Y = 2YZ^2 + 4Y^3$, and $F_Z = -X^3 + 2YZ^2$. Since we've already found all the affine singularities, we only need to look at infinity, so we set $Z = 0$. Thus, in order for $(X_0 : Y_0 : 0)$ to be a singularity, we would need

$$X_0^4 + Y_0^4 = X_0^3 = 4Y_0^3 = -X_0^3 = 0.$$

The only way this can happen is if $X_0 = Y_0 = 0$, but that's impossible in $\mathbb{P}^2$ since $Z_0$ is already 0. Thus the only singular point on $\widehat{C_f}$ is the point $(0 : 0 : 1)$. Incidentally, the picture of the cusp above is actually $C_f$.

**Exercise 4.4.** The equations of the other three curves above are $xy = x^6 + y^6$, $x^2y + xy^2 = x^4 + y^4$, and $x^2 = y^4 + x^4$. Which is which?

**Exercise 4.5.** For each of the following polynomials, find all the singular points of the corresponding projective plane curve over $\mathbb{C}$.

**a)** $f(x, y) = y^2 - x^3$

**b)** $f(x, y) = 4x^2y^2 - (x^2 + y^2)^3$

**c)** $f(x, y) = y^2 - x^4 - y^4$

You might want to sketch the affine portion (over $\mathbb{R}$) of the curves of Exercise 4.5 using a computer algebra program. (The pictures above were generated using *Mathematica*.)

**Exercise 4.6.** Show that a nonsingular plane curve is *absolutely irreducible*. In other words, if $f(x, y) \in k[x, y]$ defines the nonsingular plane curve $C_f$, and if $f = gh$ for some $g, h \in \bar{k}[x, y]$ where $\bar{k}$ is the algebraic closure of $k$, then either $g \in \bar{k}$ or $h \in \bar{k}$.

**Exercise 4.7.** Let $k$ be a field. For arbitrary $a, b \in k$, consider the projective plane curve defined by the polynomial $F(X, Y, Z) = X^3 + aXZ^2 + bZ^3 - Y^2Z$.

    **a)** If the characteristic of $k$ is not 2, for which values of $a, b$ is the curve singular?

    **b)** What happens if $k$ has characteristic 2?

## 4.2. Genus

Topologically, every nonsingular curve over $\mathbb{C}$ can be realized as a surface in $\mathbb{R}^3$. For example, an *elliptic curve* has an equation of the form $y^2 = f(x)$, where $f(x)$ is a cubic polynomial in $x$ with no repeated roots, and can be thought of as a torus (a donut) in $\mathbb{R}^3$. In general, every nonsingular curve can be realized as a torus with some number of holes, and that number of holes is called the *topological genus* of the curve. In particular, an elliptic curve has genus 1. In general, it turns out that if $f(x, y)$ is a polynomial of degree $d$ such that the curve $\widehat{C_f}$ is nonsingular, then the topological genus of $C_f$ is given by the formula $g = (d-1)(d-2)/2$. This formula is called the Plücker formula. Of course, this discussion is not rigorous. It is intended only to motivate the following definition:

**Definition 4.8.** Let $f(x, y) \in k[x, y]$ be a polynomial of degree $d$ such that $\widehat{C_f}$ is nonsingular, then the *genus* of $C_f$ (or of $\widehat{C_f}$) is defined to be

$$g := \frac{(d-1)(d-2)}{2}.$$

In other words, we have defined the genus to be what the Plücker formula gives. Although the genus of a singular curve can also be defined, we choose not to do so here.

**Exercise 4.9.** For each of the following polynomials, check that the corresponding projective plane curve is nonsingular and then find the genus of the curve.

**a)** $f(x, y) = y^2 - p(x)$, where $p(x) \in k[x]$ is of degree three with no repeated roots, and the characteristic of $k$ is not 2.

**b)** $f(x, y) = y^2 + y - p(x)$, where $p(x) \in k[x]$ is of degree three with no repeated roots, and the characteristic of $k$ is 2.

**c)** $f(x, y) = x^{q+1} + y^{q+1} - 1 \in \mathbb{F}_{q^2}[x]$, where $q$ is a prime power.

# Chapter 5

# Points, Functions, and Divisors on Curves

**Definition 5.1.** Let $k$ be a field, and let $C$ be the projective plane curve defined by $F = 0$, where $F = F(X, Y, Z) \in k[X, Y, Z]$ is a homogeneous polynomial. For any field $K$ containing $k$, we define a *$K$-rational point* on $C$ to be a point $(X_0 : Y_0 : Z_0) \in \mathbb{P}^2(K)$ such that $F(X_0, Y_0, Z_0) = 0$. The set of all $K$-rational points on $C$ is denoted $C(K)$. Elements of $C(k)$ are called *points of degree one* or simply *rational points*.

For example, if $C$ is defined by $X^2 + Y^2 = Z^2$, then $(3 : 4 : 5) = (3/5 : 4/5 : 1) \in C(\mathbb{Q}) \subset C(\mathbb{C})$, while $(3 : 2i : \sqrt{5}) = (3/\sqrt{5} : 2i/\sqrt{5} : 1)$ and $(3 : -2i : \sqrt{5}) = (3/\sqrt{5} : -2i/\sqrt{5} : 1)$ are in $C(\mathbb{C})$ but not in $C(\mathbb{Q})$.

Recall that complex solutions to equations over $\mathbb{R}$ must come in conjugate pairs. In other words, if $(x, y) = (a + bi, c + di)$ satisfies the polynomial equation $f(x, y) = 0$ where $f(x, y) \in \mathbb{R}[x, y]$, then $(a - bi, c - di)$ must also. This is essentially because complex conjugation is an automorphism of $\mathbb{C}$ which fixes $\mathbb{R}$. We may think of $(a + bi, c + di)$ and $(a - bi, c - di)$ together of defining a single point of $C_f$, but that point is of "degree two" over $\mathbb{R}$. Let's now make this idea precise for finite fields.

Assume $k = \mathbb{F}_q$ is a finite field, and pick $n \geq 1$. Recall from Appendix B that, up to isomorphism, there is a unique field $K = \mathbb{F}_{q^n}$ with $q^n$ elements. Further, $\mathbb{F}_q \subset \mathbb{F}_{q^n}$ and we have the *Frobenius automorphism* $\sigma_{q,n} : \mathbb{F}_{q^n} \to \mathbb{F}_{q^n}$ given by $\sigma_{q,n}(\alpha) = \alpha^q$. If $C$ is a projective plane curve defined over $\mathbb{F}_q$, we can let this map act on the set $C(\mathbb{F}_{q^n})$ by declaring

$$\sigma_{q,n}((X_0 : Y_0 : Z_0)) = (X_0^q : Y_0^q : Z_0^q).$$

Similarly, if $C$ is affine and $(x_0, y_0) \in C(\mathbb{F}_q)$, we define

$$\sigma_{q,n}((x_0, y_0)) = (x_0^q, y_0^q).$$

**Exercise 5.2.** Recall that $(X_0 : Y_0 : Z_0)$ is actually an equivalence class of points in $\mathbb{F}_{q^n}^3 \setminus \{(0,0,0)\}$. Show that if $(X_0 : Y_0 : Z_0) = (X_1 : Y_1 : Z_1)$, then $(X_0^q : Y_0^q : Z_0^q) = (X_1^q : Y_1^q : Z_1^q)$.

**Exercise 5.3.** Let $f(x, y) \in \mathbb{F}_q[x, y]$ and suppose that $x_0, y_0 \in \mathbb{F}_q$ satisfy the equation $f(x_0, y_0) = 0$. Show that $f(\sigma_{q,n}(x_0, y_0)) = 0$ as well.

**Definition 5.4.** Let $C$ be a nonsingular projective plane curve. A *point of degree $n$* on $C$ over $\mathbb{F}_q$ is a set $P = \{P_0, \ldots, P_{n-1}\}$ of $n$ distinct points in $C(\mathbb{F}_{q^n})$ such that $P_i = \sigma_{q,n}^i(P_0)$ for $i = 1, \ldots, n-1$.

It is not hard to see that if $C$ and $C'$ are curves defined over $\mathbb{F}_q$ by polynomials of degrees $d$ and $e$ respectively, then the $de$ points of intersection in $\mathbb{P}^2(\overline{\mathbb{F}}_q)$ guaranteed by Bezout's theorem (Theorem 3.11) cluster into points of varying degrees over $\mathbb{F}_q$, with the sum of those degrees being $de$.

As an example of a curve with points of higher degree, let $C_0$ be the projective plane curve over $\mathbb{F}_3$ corresponding to the affine equation $y^2 = x^3 + 2x + 2$.

**Exercise 5.5.** Check that $C_0$ is nonsingular and show that it has genus 1.

By plugging in the values $0, 1, 2$ for $x$, we see that there are no $\mathbb{F}_3$-rational affine points on $C$. However, homogenizing gives the equation $Y^2 Z = X^3 + 2XZ^2 + 2Z^3$ and we see that there is a unique point $P_\infty := (0 : 1 : 0)$ at infinity. Thus $C_0(\mathbb{F}_3) = \{P_\infty\}$.

Since $t^2+1$ is irreducible over $\mathbb{F}_3$, we can write $\mathbb{F}_9 = \mathbb{F}_3[t]/(t^2+1)$. Letting $\alpha$ be the element of $\mathbb{F}_9$ corresponding to $t$, we have $\mathbb{F}_9 = \{a+b\alpha \mid a,b \in \mathbb{F}_3\}$, where $\alpha^2 = -1 = 2$. Some computations yield

$$C_0(\mathbb{F}_9) = \{(0:\alpha:1),(0:2\alpha:1),(1:\alpha:1),(1:2\alpha:1),(2:\alpha:1),$$
$$(2,2\alpha:1),P_\infty\}.$$

The Frobenius $\sigma_{3,2}:\mathbb{F}_9 \to \mathbb{F}_9$ satisfies $\sigma_{3,2}(\alpha) = \alpha^3 = \alpha\cdot\alpha^2 = 2\alpha$, so we see that $C_0(\mathbb{F}_9) = Q_1 \cup Q_2 \cup Q_3 \cup \{P_\infty\}$, where $Q_1 = \{(0:\alpha:1),(0:2\alpha:1)\}$, $Q_2 = \{(1:\alpha:1),(1:2\alpha:1)\}$, and $Q_3 = \{(2:\alpha:1),(2:2\alpha:1)\}$ are the only three points of degree two on $C_0$.

Similarly, writing $\mathbb{F}_{27} = \mathbb{F}_3[t]/(t^3+2t+2)$ and letting $\omega$ be the element of $\mathbb{F}_{27}$ corresponding to $t$, we have $\mathbb{F}_{27} = \{a+b\omega+c\omega^2 \mid a,b,c \in \mathbb{F}_3\}$ and $\omega^3 = -2-2\omega = 1+\omega$. Thus, we have

$$C_0(\mathbb{F}_{27}) = \{(\omega:0:1),(1+\omega:0:1),(2+\omega:0:1),(2\omega:1:1),$$
$$(2+2\omega:1:1),(1+2\omega:1:1),(2\omega:2:1),$$
$$(2+2\omega:2:1),(1+2\omega:2:1),(2\omega^2:1+\omega^2:1),$$
$$(2+\omega+2\omega^2:2+2\omega+\omega^2:1),$$
$$(2+2\omega+2\omega^2:2+\omega+\omega^2:1),(2\omega^2:2+2\omega^2:1),$$
$$(2+\omega+2\omega^2:1+\omega+2\omega^2:1),$$
$$(2+2\omega+2\omega^2:1+2\omega+2\omega^2:1),$$
$$(1+2\omega^2:1+\omega^2:1),(\omega+2\omega^2:2+2\omega+\omega^2:1),$$
$$(2\omega+2\omega^2:2+\omega+\omega^2:1),(1+2\omega^2:2+2\omega^2:1),$$
$$(\omega+2\omega^2:1+\omega+2\omega^2:1),$$
$$(2\omega+2\omega^2:1+2\omega+2\omega^2:1),$$
$$(2+2\omega^2:1+\omega^2:1),(1+\omega+2\omega^2:2+2\omega+\omega^2:1),$$
$$(1+2\omega+2\omega^2:2+\omega+\omega^2:1),(2+2\omega^2:2+2\omega^2:1),$$
$$(1+\omega+2\omega^2:1+\omega+2\omega^2:1),$$
$$(1+2\omega+2\omega^2:1+2\omega+2\omega^2:1),P_\infty\}$$

The Frobenius $\sigma_{3,3}:\mathbb{F}_{27} \to \mathbb{F}_{27}$ satisfies $\sigma_{3,3}(\omega) = \omega^3 = 1+\omega$, so we see that $\mathbb{C}_0(\mathbb{F}_{27}) = R_1 \cup R_2 \cup \cdots \cup R_9 \cup \{P_\infty\}$ where $R_1,\ldots,R_9$ are the nine points of degree three on $C_0$. For example, we could take $R_1 = \{(\omega : 0 : 1), \sigma_{3,3}((\omega : 0 : 1)), \sigma_{3,3}^2((\omega : 0 : 1))\} = \{(\omega : 0 : 1), (1 + \omega : 0 : 1), (2 + \omega : 0 : 1)\}$.

**Exercise 5.6.** Let $C$ be the projective plane curve defined by the equation $Y^q Z + Y Z^q = X^{q+1}$ over the field $\mathbb{F}_{q^2}$, where $q$ is a power of a prime. $C$ is called a *Hermitian curve*.

a) Show that $C$ is nonsingular and compute the genus of $C$.

b) Set $q = 2$ and find $C(\mathbb{F}_4)$.

c) For an arbitrary prime power $q$, show that there is a unique point at infinity on $C$.

d) Again for an arbitrary prime power $q$, prove that $\#C(\mathbb{F}_{q^2}) = q^3 + 1$.

We remarked earlier that if $C$ and $C'$ are two projective plane curves over $\mathbb{F}_q$ defined by polynomials of degrees $d$ and $e$ respectively, then the set of points over $\bar{\mathbb{F}}_q$ in which they intersect will cluster into points $P_1, P_2, \ldots, P_\ell$ of varying degrees over $\mathbb{F}_q$, where a point is listed more than once if the intersection of the two curves is with multiplicity greater than one there. Further, we have $de = r_1 + r_2 + \cdots + r_\ell$, where $r_i$ is the degree of the point $P_i$ over $\mathbb{F}_q$. To express this, we might write $C \cap C' = P_1 + \cdots + P_\ell$ and call $C \cap C'$ the *intersection divisor* of $C$ and $C'$. With this motivation, we make the following definition:

**Definition 5.7.** Let $C$ be a curve defined over $\mathbb{F}_q$. A *divisor* $D$ on $C$ over $\mathbb{F}_q$ is an element of the free abelian group on the set of points (of arbitrary degree) on $C$ over $\mathbb{F}_q$. Thus, every divisor is of the form $D = \sum n_Q Q$, where the $n_Q$ are integers and each $Q$ is a point (of arbitrary degree) on $C$. If $n_Q \geq 0$ for all $Q$, we call $D$ *effective* and write $D \geq 0$. We define the *degree* of the divisor $D = \sum n_Q Q$ to be $\deg D = \sum n_Q \deg Q$. Finally, the *support* of the divisor $D = \sum n_Q Q$ is $\mathrm{supp} D = \{Q \mid n_Q \neq 0\}$.

Note that the support of $D$ is always a finite set and that the intersection divisor $C \cap C'$ introduced above is an effective divisor of degree $de$.

Let's now return to our example where $C_0$ is the projective plane curve defined over $\mathbb{F}_3$ corresponding to the affine equation $y^2 = x^3 +$

$2x + 2$. If we set $D = 5P_\infty - 2Q_3 + 7R_1$, then $D$ is a divisor on $C_0$ over $\mathbb{F}_3$ of degree $5(1) - 2(2) + 7(3) = 22$ with support $\{P_\infty, Q_3, R_1\}$. Note that $(0 : \alpha : 1) + (\omega : 0 : 1)$ is *not* a divisor on $C_0$ over $\mathbb{F}_3$ since $(0 : \alpha : 1)$ and $(\omega : 0 : 1)$ are not points on $C_0$ over $\mathbb{F}_3$.

**Definition 5.8.** Let $F(X, Y, Z)$ be the polynomial which defines the nonsingular projective plane curve $C$ over the field $\mathbb{F}_q$. The *field of rational functions on $C$* is

$$\mathbb{F}_q(C) := \left( \left\{ \frac{g(X, Y, Z)}{h(X, Y, Z)} \;\middle|\; \begin{array}{c} g, h \in \mathbb{F}_q[X, Y, Z] \\ \text{are homogeneous} \\ \text{of the same degree} \end{array} \right\} \cup \{0\} \right) / \sim$$

where $g/h \sim g'/h'$ if and only if $gh' - g'h \in \langle F \rangle \subset \mathbb{F}_q[X, Y, Z]$.

**Exercise 5.9.** Show that $\mathbb{F}_q(C)$ is indeed a field and that it contains $\mathbb{F}_q$ as a subfield.

Returning again to our example of the curve $C_0$ defined over $\mathbb{F}_3$, we have $F(X, Y, Z) = Y^2 Z - X^3 - 2XZ^2 - 2Z^3$. We see that $X^2/Z^2$ and $(Y^2 + XZ + Z^2)/XZ$ are the same element of $\mathbb{F}_3(C_0)$ since

$$(X^2)(XZ) - (Z^2)(Y^2 + XZ + Z^2) = 2Z(Y^2 Z - X^3 - 2XZ^2 - 2Z^3)$$

in $\mathbb{F}_3[X, Y, Z]$.

Let us now return to our general discussion. Let $C$ be a projective plane curve defined over $\mathbb{F}_q$, and let $f := g/h \in \mathbb{F}_q(C)$. By Bezout's theorem (Theorem 3.11), we have that the curves defined by $g = 0$ and $h = 0$ each intersect $C$ in exactly $de$ points of $\mathbb{P}^2(\bar{k})$, where $d$ is the degree of the polynomial defining $C$ and $e = \deg g = \deg h$.

**Definition 5.10.** Let $C$ be a curve defined over $\mathbb{F}_q$ and let $f := g/h \in \mathbb{F}_q(C)$. The *divisor of $f$* is defined to be $\operatorname{div}(f) := \sum P - \sum Q$, where $\sum P$ is the intersection divisor $C \cap C_g$ and $\sum Q$ is the intersection divisor $C \cap C_h$.

Let $f = g/h$ be a rational function on $C$. Then intuitively, the points where $C$ and the curve defined by $g$ intersect are the *zeros* of $f$ and the points where $C$ and the curve defined by $h$ intersect are the *poles* of $f$, so we think of $\operatorname{div}(f)$ as being "the zeros of $f$ minus the poles of $f$". Since $\deg(C \cap C_g) = \deg(C \cap C_h) = de$, we have $\deg \operatorname{div}(f) = 0$. Intuitively, $f$ has the same number of zeros as poles. Note that if $P$ appears in both $C \cap C_g$ and $C \cap C_h$, then some cancellation will occur. In particular, $P$ is only considered to be a zero (resp., pole) of $f$ if after the cancellation, $P$ still appears in $\text{div}(f)$ with positive (resp., negative) coefficient. Notice also that the divisor of a constant function $f \in \mathbb{F}_q \subset \mathbb{F}_q(C)$ is just 0.

Since rational functions are actually equivalence classes, we need to be sure that our definition of $\text{div}(f)$ is independent of the choice of representative for the equivalence class of $f$. It is, but the proof is messy. Instead, we'll just illustrate this in our example. On our curve $C_0$ over $\mathbb{F}_3$ defined by $Y^2 Z - X^3 - 2XZ^2 - 2Z^3 = 0$, we need to compute the intersection divisor of $C_0$ with the curves defined by each of the following equations: $X^2 = 0$, $Z^2 = 0$, $Y^2 + Z^2 + XZ = 0$, and $XZ = 0$. Any point $(X_0 : Y_0 : Z_0)$ of intersection between the line $X = 0$ and the curve $C_0$ must satisfy $X_0 = 0$ and $Z_0(Y_0^2 - 2Z_0^2)$. Writing $\mathbb{F}_9 = \mathbb{F}_3[t]/(t^2 + 1)$ and letting $\alpha$ denote the element of $\mathbb{F}_9$ corresponding to $t$, we have that $\alpha^2 = -1 = 2$, so the polynomial $(Y_0^2 - 2Z_0)^2$ factors as $(Y - \alpha Z)(Y + \alpha Z)$. This means that our point $(X_0 : Y_0 : Z_0)$ must satisfy $X_0 = 0$ and one of the following three conditions: $Z_0 = 0$, $Y_0 = \alpha Z_0$, or $Y_0 = 2\alpha Z_0$. Thus our three points of intersection in $\mathbb{P}^2(\mathbb{F}_9)$ are $P_\infty$, $(0 : \alpha : 1)$ and $(0 : 2\alpha : 1)$. Since $\{(0 : \alpha : 1), (0 : 2\alpha : 1)\}$ is our point $Q_1$ from before, we have that the intersection divisor of the line $X = 0$ with $C_0$ is $P_\infty + Q_1$. Therefore, the intersection divisor of the "double line" $X^2 = 0$ and the curve $C_0$ is $2P_\infty + 2Q_1$. Notice that this divisor does indeed have degree $6 = 2 \cdot 3$.

**Exercise 5.11.** Show that the intersection divisor of $C_0$ with the curve defined by $Z^2 = 0$ is $6P_\infty$. Show that the intersection divisor of $C_0$ with the curve defined by $XZ = 0$ is $4P_\infty + Q_1$.

The intersection of $C_0$ with the curve defined by $Y^2 + Z^2 + XZ = 0$ is a little trickier to compute since this latter curve is not just the union of two lines. However, the only point at infinity on the latter curve is $(1 : 0 : 0)$ and the only point at infinity on $C_0$ is $P_\infty = (0 : 1 : 0)$, so the two curves do not intersect at infinity. Thus we may assume $Z \neq 0$, divide through by $Z^2$, and set $x = X/Z$, $y = Y/Z$ to get the affine portion of $C_0$ defined by $y^2 - x^3 - 2x - 2 = 0$ and the other curve defined by $y^2 + 1 + x = 0$. We still don't have a product of two lines, but we can write $x = -(1+y^2)$ from the second equation and substitute that in. We have $0 = y^2 + (1 + y^2)^3 + 2(1 + y^2) + 2 = y^6 + 1 = (y^2 + 1)^3 = (y - \alpha)^3 (y + \alpha)^3$. Thus these two curves intersect with multiplicity 3 at $Q_1$, so the intersection divisor is $3Q_1$.

Putting the results of the last two paragraphs and the exercise in between them together, we have $\operatorname{div}(X^2/Z^2) = (2P_\infty + 2Q_1) - 6P_\infty = 2Q_1 - 4P_\infty$ and $\operatorname{div}((Y^2 + XZ + Z^2)/XZ) = 3Q_1 - (4P_\infty + Q_1) = 2Q_1 - 4P_\infty$, so the two divisors do indeed agree.

Now that we know what divisors, rational functions, and divisors of rational functions are, we are ready for our next definition.

**Definition 5.12.** Let $D$ be a divisor on the nonsingular projective plane curve $C$ defined over the field $\mathbb{F}_q$. Then the *space of rational functions associated to $D$* is

$$L(D) := \{f \in \mathbb{F}_q(C) \mid \operatorname{div}(f) + D \geq 0\} \cup \{0\}.$$

A few comments are in order. First, it's easy to see that $L(D)$ is a vector space over $\mathbb{F}_q$. In fact, it's finite dimensional, but this is harder. By collecting positive and negative coefficients appearing in the divisor $D$, we can write $D = D_{pos} - D_{neg}$, where $D_{pos}$ and $D_{neg}$ are effective divisors. Also, we can write $\operatorname{div}(f)$ as a difference of two effective divisors by saying $\operatorname{div}(f) = $ (zeros of $f$) $-$ (poles of $f$) . Therefore, we have $\operatorname{div}(f) + D = (D_{pos} - $ (poles of $f$) $) + ($ (zeros of $f$) $- D_{neg})$. Intuitively, then, $f \in \mathbb{F}_q(C)$ is in $L(D)$ if and only if $f$ has "enough" zeros and "not too many" poles.

**Exercise 5.13.** Let $D$ be a divisor on a nonsingular projective plane curve $C$ defined over the field $\mathbb{F}_q$.

  **a)** Show that if $\deg D \leq 0$ then $L(D) = \{0\}$.

  **b)** Show that $\mathbb{F}_q \subset L(D)$ if and only if $D \geq 0$.

We close this chapter with a statement of the important theorem of Riemann and Roch:

**Theorem 5.14.** (Riemann-Roch Theorem) *Let $C$ be a nonsingular projective plane curve of genus $g$ defined over the field $\mathbb{F}_q$ and let $D$ be a divisor on $X$. Then $\dim L(D) \geq \deg D + 1 - g$. Further, if*

$\deg D > 2g - 2$, *then*

$$\dim L(D) = \deg D + 1 - g.$$

Let us return one final time to our ongoing example. We have the curve $C_0$ defined over $\mathbb{F}_3$ by the equation $Y^2 Z - X^3 - 2XZ^2 - 2Z^3$. Recall that $Q_1$ is the point $\{(0 : \alpha : 1), (0 : 2\alpha : 1)\}$ of degree 2 on $C_0$, where $\alpha^2 + 1 = 0$. We can put the results above together to see that the divisor of the rational function $X/Z$ on $C_0$ is $Q_1 - 2P_\infty$. Further, it is easy to check that the divisor of the rational function $Y/Z$ is $R_1 - 3P_\infty$, where $R_1$ is the point $\{(\omega : 0 : 1), (1+\omega : 0 : 1), (2+\omega : 0 : 1)\}$ of degree three on $C_0$ with $\omega \in \mathbb{F}_{27}$ satisfying $\omega^3 = 1 + \omega$. Thus, for any $i, j \geq 0$, we have $\operatorname{div}(X^i Y^j / Z^{i+j}) = iQ_1 + jR_1 - (2i + 3j)P_\infty$.

Now let $r$ be a positive integer and set $D = rP_\infty$. Using the Riemann-Roch Theorem and Exercise 5.5, we know that $\dim L(D) = \deg(D) + 1 - g = r + 1 - 1 = r$. When $r = 1$, we have $\mathbb{F}_q = L(D)$ by Exercise 5.13, so $\{1\}$ is a basis for $L(D)$. When $r = 2$, we have $X/Z \in L(D)$ by the previous paragraph, and since $\{1, X/Z\}$ is clearly linearly independent, it must be a basis for $L(D)$. When $r = 3$, we see that $\operatorname{div}(Y/Z) + D = R_1 - 3P_\infty + 3P_\infty = R_1 \geq 0$ and so $\{1, X/Z, Y/Z\}$ is a basis for $L(D)$.

**Exercise 5.15.** Let $C_1$ be the projective elliptic curve defined by the equation $Y^2 Z + YZ^2 = X^3 + XZ^2 + Z^3$ over $\mathbb{F}_2$.

   **a)** Check that $C_1$ is nonsingular and has genus 1.

   **b)** Find all points of degree 1, 2, 3, and 4 on $C_1$ over $\mathbb{F}_2$.

   **c)** Find $\operatorname{div}(f)$ for each of the following rational functions on $C_1$:
   $1, X/Z, Y/Z, X^2/Z^2, XY/Z^2$.

   **d)** Letting $P_\infty$ denote the unique point at infinity on $C_1$, Find a basis for $L(rP_\infty)$ for $r = 0, 1, 2, 3, 4, 5$.

   **e)** Find $\operatorname{div}(X^i Y^j / Z^{i+j})$, where $i$ and $j$ are arbitrary nonnegative integers.

   **f)** For an arbitrary nonnegative integer $r$, find a basis for $L(rP_\infty)$.

# Chapter 6

# Algebraic Geometry Codes

In this chapter we put our understanding of codes together with our understanding of algebraic geometry to describe Goppa's construction of algebraic geometric codes. To avoid confusion, the letter $C$ will be reserved in this chapter to refer to codes, while the letter $X$ will be used for curves. Also, we will be always be working over the finite field $\mathbb{F}_q$, so the symbol $k$ can unambiguously be used to denote a positive integer (the dimension of a code) as in the earlier chapters on coding theory.

Recall the definition of the Reed-Solomon Codes (Definition 1.8): We let $L_{k-1}$ be the set of polynomials $f \in \mathbb{F}_q[x]$ of degree at most $k - 1$ (plus the zero polynomial). Then $L_{k-1}$ is a vector space of dimension $k$ over $\mathbb{F}_q$. If the $q - 1$ elements of $\mathbb{F}_q^\times$ are $\alpha_1, \ldots, \alpha_{q-1}$, then the Reed-Solomon code $RS(k, q)$ is defined to be

$$RS(k, q) := \{(f(\alpha_1), \ldots, f(\alpha_{q-1})) \mid f \in L_{k-1}\}.$$

Recall that the projective plane was defined as

$$\mathbb{P}^2(\mathbb{F}_q) = (\mathbb{F}_q^3 \setminus \{(0, 0, 0)\})/ \sim,$$

where $(X_0, Y_0, Z_0) \sim (X_1, Y_1, Z_1)$ if and only if there is some $\alpha \in k^\times$ with $X_1 = \alpha X_0$, $Y_1 = \alpha Y_0$, and $Z_1 = \alpha Z_0$. In the same spirit, we have:

**Definition 6.1.** The *projective line* $\mathbb{P}^1(\mathbb{F}_q)$ is defined to be

$$(\mathbb{F}_q^2 \setminus \{(0,0)\})/\sim,$$

where $(X_0, Y_0) \sim (X_1, Y_1)$ if and only if there is some $\alpha \in \mathbb{F}_q^\times$ with $X_1 = \alpha X_0$ and $Y_1 = \alpha Y_0$.

Writing $(X_0 : Y_0)$ for the equivalence class of the point $(X_0, Y_0)$, we have that

$$\mathbb{P}^1(\mathbb{F}_q) = \{(\alpha : 1) \,|\, \alpha \in \mathbb{F}_q\} \cup \{(1 : 0)\}$$

We may think of $\mathbb{P}_1$ as the line defined by the equation $Z = 0$ in $\mathbb{P}^2$. It is a curve of genus 0.

**Exercise 6.2.** Writing $P_\infty$ for the point $(1 : 0)$, set $D = (k-1)P_\infty$. Show that $L(D) = L_{k-1}$ (where we identify a polynomial $f(x) \in \mathbb{F}_q[x]$ of degree $d$ with its homogenization $Y^d f(X/Y) \in \mathbb{F}_q[X, Y]$).

If we set $P_i = (\alpha_i : 1)$ (using the numbering of the elements of $\mathbb{F}_q^\times$ as above), we have the following alternate description of the Reed-Solomon code:

$$RS(k, q) = \{(f(P_1), \ldots, f(P_n)) \,|\, f \in L((k-1)P_\infty)\}$$

Goppa's idea [**Go**] was to generalize this. Let $X$ be a projective, nonsingular plane curve over $\mathbb{F}_q$, and let $D$ be a divisor on $X$. Let $\mathcal{P} = \{P_1, \ldots, P_n\} \subset X(\mathbb{F}_q)$ be a set of $n$ distinct $\mathbb{F}_q$-rational points on $X$. If we assume that $\mathcal{P} \cap \mathrm{supp}\,D = \emptyset$, then no $P_i$ can be a pole of any $f \in L(D)$, and, in fact, $f(P_i) \in \mathbb{F}_q$ for any $f \in L(D)$ and any $P_i \in \mathcal{P}$.

**Definition 6.3.** Let $X$, $\mathcal{P}$, and $D$ be as above. Then the *algebraic geometric code* associated to $X$, $\mathcal{P}$, and $D$ is

$$C(X, \mathcal{P}, D) := \{(f(P_1), \ldots, f(P_n)) \,|\, f \in L(D)\} \subset \mathbb{F}_q^n.$$

In other words, the algebraic geometric code $C(X, \mathcal{P}, D)$ is the image of the *evaluation map*

$$\epsilon : L(D) \to \mathbb{F}_q^n$$
$$f \mapsto (f(P_1), \ldots, f(P_n))$$

Since $L(D)$ is a vector space over $\mathbb{F}_q$ and the evaluation map $\epsilon$ is a linear transformation, we see that $C(X, \mathcal{P}, D)$ is a linear code. Further, its length is obviously $n = \#\mathcal{P}$. What about the dimension? Clearly, it's at most $\dim L(D)$, and it's exactly $\dim L(D)$ if and only if $\epsilon$ is one-to-one. This is true if and only if the kernel of $\epsilon$ is trivial (Exercise A.23). So suppose $\epsilon(f) = 0$. Then $f(P_1) = \cdots = f(P_n) = 0$, so the coefficient of each $P_i$ in the divisor $\operatorname{div}(f)$ is at least 1. Since no $P_i$ is in $\operatorname{supp} D$, we have that $\operatorname{div}(f) + D - P_1 - \cdots - P_n \geq 0$, which means that $f \in L(D - P_1 - \cdots - P_n)$. If we add a hypothesis that $\deg D < n$, then the divisor $D - P_1 - \cdots - P_n$ has negative degree, so its associated space of rational functions is $\{0\}$ by Exercise 5.13. This means $f = 0$, so $\dim C = \dim L(D)$. In fact, we have the following theorem:

**Theorem 6.4.** *Let $X$ be a nonsingular, projective plane curve of genus $g$, defined over the field $\mathbb{F}_q$. Let $\mathcal{P} \subset X(\mathbb{F}_q)$ be a set of $n$ distinct $\mathbb{F}_q$-rational points on $X$, and let $D$ be a divisor on $X$ satisfying $2g - 2 < \deg D < n$. Then the algebraic geometric code $C := C(X, \mathcal{P}, D)$ is linear of length $n$, dimension $k := \deg D + 1 - g$, and minimum distance $d$, where $d \geq n - \deg D$.*

**Proof.** We've already shown that $C$ is linear of length $n$ and dimension $\dim L(D)$, since $\deg D < n$. That $\dim L(D) = \deg D + 1 - g$ is exactly the statement of the Riemann-Roch Theorem, since $\deg D > 2g - 2$. To get the lower bound on the minimum distance of $C$, we use an argument similar to the one we used to compute $k$. Let $\epsilon(f) = (f(P_1), \ldots, f(P_n)) \in C$ be a codeword of minimum nonzero weight $d$. Then exactly $d$ coordinates of $\epsilon(f)$ are nonzero, so without loss of generality, we may assume $f(P_{d+1}) = \cdots = f(P_n) = 0$. As before, this means that the divisor $\operatorname{div}(f) + D - P_{d+1} - \cdots - P_n$ is effective, and by Exercise 5.13, the divisor $D - P_{d+1} - \cdots - P_n$ must have nonnegative degree. In other words, we have $\deg D - (n - d) \geq 0$, or $d \geq n - \deg D$ as desired. $\qquad\square$

Let $C = C(X, \mathcal{P}, D)$ be an algebraic geometric code and let $f_1, f_2, \ldots, f_k$ be a basis for the vector space $L(D)$ over $\mathbb{F}_q$. Under the conditions of the theorem, we know that $\dim C = k$, and so we know that $\epsilon(f_1), \epsilon(f_2), \ldots, \epsilon(f_k)$ is a basis for $C$. This means that the matrix

$$\begin{pmatrix} f_1(P_1) & f_1(P_2) & \cdots & f_1(P_n) \\ f_2(P_1) & f_2(P_2) & \cdots & f_2(P_n) \\ \vdots & \vdots & \ddots & \vdots \\ f_k(P_1) & f_k(P_2) & \cdots & f_k(P_n) \end{pmatrix}$$

is a generator matrix for $C$.

**Exercise 6.5.** Let $E$ be the projective plane curve defined by the equation $Y^2Z + YZ^2 = X^3 + XZ^2 + Z^3$ over the field $\mathbb{F}_2$. (This is the same curve we studied in Exercise 5.15.) Let $\mathcal{P} = E(\mathbb{F}_8) \setminus \{P_\infty\}$. Let $C$ be the algebraic geometric code $C = C(E, \mathcal{P}, 5P_\infty)$, defined over $\mathbb{F}_8$.

    **a)** What do the theoretical results say about the parameters of $C$?

    **b)** Find a generator matrix for $C$.

    **c)** Determine the exact parameters of $C$.

**Exercise 6.6.** Recall that an MDS code is a code which meets the Singleton Bound (Theorem 2.1). Show that every algebraic geometric code defined from the projective line is MDS.

**Exercise 6.7.** (adapted from [S]) Let $\alpha = (\alpha_1, \ldots, \alpha_n)$, where the $\alpha_i$ are distinct elements of $\mathbb{F}_q$, let $v = (v_1, \ldots, v_n)$ where the $v_i$ are nonzero (not necessarily distinct) elements of $\mathbb{F}_q$, and let $k$ be a fixed integer, $1 \le k \le n$. The *Generalized Reed-Solomon code* is defined to be

$$GRS_k(\alpha, v) := \{v_1 f(\alpha_1), \ldots, v_n f(\alpha_n) \mid f \in L_{k-1}\}.$$

Here, as before, $L_{k-1}$ denotes the $k$-dimensional $\mathbb{F}_q$-vector space of polynomials over $\mathbb{F}_q$ of degree at most $k - 1$.

    **a)** Find values for $\alpha$ and $v$ so that $GRS_k(\alpha, v) = RS(k, q)$.

    **b)** Show that there is a polynomial $u = u(z) \in \mathbb{F}_q[z]$ satisfying $u(\alpha_i) = v_i$ for $i = 1, \ldots, n$.

    **c)** Find $\text{div}(u)$.

    **d)** Show that there is a set $\mathcal{P} \subset \mathbb{P}_1(\mathbb{F}_q)$ and a divisor $D$ on $\mathbb{P}_1$ such that $GRS_k(\alpha, v) = C(\mathbb{P}_1, \mathcal{P}, D)$.

# Chapter 7

# Good Codes from Algebraic Geometry

Now that we understand Goppa's construction of algebraic geometric codes, let's investigate the result of Tsfasman, Vladut, and Zink. Recall that in 1982, just after Goppa ([**Go**]) announced his construction in 1977, Tsfasman, Vladut, and Zink ([**TVZ**]) proved that there was a sequence of algebraic geometric codes which had parameters which were better than those guaranteed by the Asymptotic Gilbert-Varshamov Bound (Theorem 2.9).

We begin by exploring the asymptotic parameters of algebraic geometric codes. Let $C = C(X, \mathcal{P}, D)$ be an algebraic geometric code, where $X$ is a curve of genus $g$ defined over $\mathbb{F}_q$, $\mathcal{P}$ is a set of $\mathbb{F}_q$-rational points on $X$ of size $n := \#\mathcal{P}$, and $D$ is a divisor on $X$ satisfying $2g - 2 < \deg D < n$. Theorem 6.4 tells us that $C$ is a linear code of length $n$, dimension $k$, and minimum distance $d \geq n - \deg D$. Thus the information rate $R$ of $C$ is $k/n = (\deg D + 1 - g)/n$ and the relative minimum distance $\delta$ of $C$ is $d/n \geq (n - \deg D)/n$. One way of thinking about the fact that we want both $R$ and $\delta$ large while acknowledging that there is a trade-off between these values is to say that we want $R + \delta$ large. In our situation, we have

$$R + \delta \geq \frac{\deg D + 1 - g}{n} + \frac{n - \deg D}{n} = \frac{n + 1 - g}{n} = 1 + 1/n - g/n.$$

For long codes, we consider the limit as $n$ gets large. This means we consider a sequence of algebraic geometric codes of increasing length. To construct these codes, we need a sequence of curves $X_i$ of genus $g_i$, a set of $n_i$ rational points on $X_i$, and a chosen divisor $D_i$ on $X_i$. Then, we obtain

$$\lim_{n \to \infty} (R + \delta) \geq 1 - \lim_{i \to \infty} g_i / n_i.$$

Since we want $R + \delta$ to be big, we want $\lim_{n \to \infty} (g/n)$ to be small, or equivalently, we want $\lim_{n \to \infty} (n/g)$ to be as large as possible. Remembering that $n \leq \#X(\mathbb{F}_q)$ for a curve $X$ of genus $g$, we are prompted to make the following definitions:

**Definition 7.1.** Let $q$ be a prime power. Then for any nonnegative integer $g$, we define

$$N_q(g) := \max\{\#X(\mathbb{F}_q) \mid X \text{ is a curve over } \mathbb{F}_q \text{ of genus } g\}$$

and

$$A(q) := \limsup_{g \to \infty} N_q(g)/g.$$

Our question is now: What is the value of $A(q)$? Let's make sure we understand the relevance of this question. Suppose we have a sequence of curves $X_i$ defined over $\mathbb{F}_q$ satisfying $\lim_{i \to \infty} N_i/g_i = A(q)$, where $g_i$ is the genus of $X_i$ and $N_i = \#X_i(\mathbb{F}_q)$. For each $i$, pick $Q_i \in X_i(\mathbb{F}_q)$, and set $\mathcal{P}_i = X(\mathbb{F}_q) \setminus \{Q_i\}$. Also pick positive integers $r_i$ with $2g_i - 2 < r_i < N_i - 1 = \mathcal{P}_i$. Then the algebraic geometric code $C_i = C(X, \mathcal{P}_i, r_i Q_i)$ has length $N_i - 1$, dimension $r_i + 1 - g_i$, and minimum distance at least $N_i - 1 - r_i$. If $R_i$ is the information rate of $C_i$ and $\delta_i$ is the relative minimum distance of $C_i$, then we have

$$R_i + \delta_i \geq 1 + 1/(N_i - 1) - g_i/(N_i - 1).$$

Setting $R := \lim_{i \to \infty} R_i$ and $\delta := \lim_{i \to \infty} \delta_i$, we have

$$R + \delta \geq 1 - 1/A(q)$$

Thus, recalling the definition

$$\alpha_q(\delta) := \limsup_{n \to \infty} \frac{1}{n} \log_q A_q(n, \delta n),$$

we have proven that $\alpha_q(\delta) \geq -\delta + 1 - 1/A(q)$. Since the equation $R = -\delta + 1 - 1/A(q)$ defines a line of negative slope, it will intersect the

Gilbert-Varshamov curve (the graph of $R = 1 - H_q(\delta)$) in either 0, 1, or 2 points. If it intersects in two points, then we have an improvement on the Gilbert-Varshamov bound in the interval between those two points.

Thus, we are back to the question of the value of $A(q)$. Non-asymptotically, the question is: How many rational points can a curve of genus $g$ have? To get a feel for things, let's investigate this first. If we restrict ourselves to plane curves, as we've done in this course, then the number of rational points is clearly bounded by $\#\mathbb{P}^2(\mathbb{F}_q) = q^2 + q + 1$. However, not every curve is a plane curve, and we can get curves with many more rational points by removing this restriction. In this more general setting, the fundamental result in the area is:

**Theorem 7.2.** (Hasse-Weil) *Let $X$ be a nonsingular projective curve of genus $g$ over the field $\mathbb{F}_q$ and set $N = \#X(\mathbb{F}_q)$. Then*

$$|N - (q+1)| \le 2g\sqrt{q}.$$

A curve with exactly $q + 1 + 2g\sqrt{q}$ rational points is called *maximal*. Clearly, maximal curves can only exist over fields with cardinality a perfect square, and if $q$ is not a perfect square, we can certainly replace the right-hand side of the above inequality with $\lfloor 2g\sqrt{q} \rfloor$. With work, we can do a little better:

**Theorem 7.3.** (Serre) *In the situation of Theorem 7.2, one has*

$$|N - (q+1)| \le g\lfloor 2\sqrt{q} \rfloor.$$

**Exercise 7.4.** Show that the Hermitian curve (Exercise 5.6) is maximal, and compute the theoretical parameters of $C(X, \mathcal{P}, D)$ where $\mathcal{P} = X(\mathbb{F}_{q^2}) \setminus \{P_\infty\}$ and $D = rP_\infty$ for appropriate values of $r$.

Unfortunately, the improvement of Theorem 7.3 isn't enough to guarantee that curves meeting the bound exist. In fact, it can be shown that the bound of Theorem 7.3 cannot be met if $g > (q-\sqrt{q})/2$. Better bounds do exist for curves of large genus, but they're quite messy.

Finally, let's return to the asymptotic question of the value of $A(q)$. There is the following upper bound on $A(q)$:

**Theorem 7.5.** (Drinfeld-Vladut, [**VD**]) *For any prime power $q$, we have $A(q) \leq \sqrt{q} - 1$.*

On the other hand, the following result is due to Tsfasman, Vladut, and Zink in the cases $m = 1$ and $m = 2$, and to Ihara in general:

**Theorem 7.6.** ([**I**], [**TVZ**]) *Let $q = p^{2m}$ be an even power of the prime $p$. Then there is a sequence of curves $X_i$ defined over $\mathbb{F}_q$ having genus $g_i$ and $N_i$ rational points such that*

$$\lim_{i \to \infty} N_i / g_i = \sqrt{q} - 1.$$

The curves $X_i$ are *modular* and a study of them is beyond the scope of this course. However, putting everything together, we have that $A(q) = \sqrt{q} - 1$ when $q$ is a perfect square, giving the following theorem:

**Theorem 7.7.** (Tsfasman-Vladut-Zink Bound [**TVZ**]) *Let $q$ be a perfect square. Then*

$$\alpha_q(\delta) \geq -\delta + 1 - \frac{1}{(\sqrt{q} - 1)}.$$

By doing a little computation, it's not difficult to see that the "Tsfasman-Vladut-Zink line" $R = -\delta + 1 - 1/(\sqrt{q} - 1)$ and the "Gilbert-Varshamov curve" $R = 1 - H_q(\delta)$ will intersect in exactly two points whenever $q \geq 49$. Therefore, for all perfect squares $q \geq 49$, the Tsfasman-Vladut-Zink Bound gives an improvement on the Gilbert-Varshamov bound for the possible asymptotic parameters of codes over the field $\mathbb{F}_q$.

**Exercise 7.8.** For each of the following values of $q$, draw a careful plot of the asymptotic Plotkin bound, the asymptotic Gilbert-Varshamov bound, and the Tsfasman-Vladut-Zink bound on a single set of axes: $q = 25$, $q = 49$, and $q = 64$.

# Appendix A

# Abstract Algebra Review

Throughout the course, we need some concepts which you have probably already seen in abstract algebra. The purpose of this appendix is to review those concepts. It is not intended to serve as a first introduction to abstract algebra, and the reader who has not seen this material before is referred to any of the several good undergraduate abstract algebra texts, for example [**Ga**].

## A.1. Groups

**Definition A.1.** A *group* is a set $G$ equipped with one operation, usually denoted by $\cdot$ (or concatenation). Although this operation takes on different meanings in different groups (addition, multiplication, composition of functions, etc.), it is usually called *multiplication* in the general case. Every group must satisfy the following properties:

- Existence of Identity: There is an element $e_G \in G$ such that $e_G a = a = a e_G$ for all $a \in G$.

- Associativity: For all $a, b, c \in G$, we have $(ab)c = a(bc)$.

- Existence of Inverses: For each $a \in G$, there is an element $b \in G$ such that $ab = e_G = ba$.

A few comments: First notice that multiplication need not be commutative. In fact, a group $G$ is called *abelian* if $ab = ba$ for all $a, b \in G$. Also, it's not hard to show that the identity of $G$ is unique, which is why we can unambiguously call it "$e_G$". Similarly, the inverse of each element of $G$ is unique, so we denote the inverse of $x \in G$ as $x^{-1}$. Some examples of groups are: $\mathbb{Z}$ under addition, $\mathbb{Q} \setminus \{0\}$ under multiplication, $GL_n(\mathbb{Q})$ (the set of invertible $n \times n$ matrices with entries in $\mathbb{Q}$) under matrix multiplication, $S_A$ (all the one-to-one and onto functions from a set $A$ to itself) under function composition.

A *subgroup* $H$ of a group $G$ is a subset of $G$ which is a group under the same operation as $G$. A subgroup $H$ is called *normal* if whenever $x \in G$ and $h \in H$ we have $xhx^{-1} \in H$. A *cyclic group* is a group $C$ which has an element $a$ such that $C = \{a^k \mid k \in \mathbb{Z}\}$. In this case we write $C = \langle a \rangle$. The *order* of a group is the number of elements it has. It is not difficult to show that, up to isomorphism, (see Definition A.21 below) there is only one cyclic group of order $n$ for each positive integer $n$. We will use $C_n$ to denote this group.

We'll need one theorem from finite group theory in Appendix B:

**Theorem A.2.** (Fundamental Theorem of Finite Abelian Groups) *Let $G$ be a finite abelian group. Then $G$ can be written as a direct sum of cyclic groups. In fact, there are two canonical ways of doing this:*

- *There are primes $p_1, \ldots, p_k$ and positive integers $n_1, \ldots, n_k$ such that*
$$G \cong C_{p_1^{n_1}} \oplus \cdots \oplus C_{p_k^{n_k}}$$
- *There are integers $r_1, \ldots, r_t$ with $r_{i+1}$ dividing $r_i$ for all $i$ and such that*
$$G \cong C_{r_1} \oplus \cdots \oplus C_{r_t}$$

## A.2. Rings, Fields, Ideals, and Factor Rings

**Definition A.3.** A *ring* is a set $R$ equipped with two operations, usually denoted by $+$ and $\cdot$ (or concatenation). As with the operation in a group, the meanings of these operations will vary from ring to ring, but we tend to call $+$ *addition* and $\cdot$ *multiplication* in general. Every ring must satisfy all of the following properties:

- Existence of Additive Identity: There is an element $0 \in R$ such that $0 + a = a = a + 0$ for all $a \in R$.

- Existence of Additive Inverses: For each $a \in R$, there is an element $b \in R$ such that $a + b = 0 = b + a$.

- Commutativity of Addition: For all $a, b \in R$ we have $a + b = b + a$.

- Associativity of Addition: For all $a, b, c \in R$ we have $(a+b)+c = a + (b + c)$

- Existence of Multiplicative Identity: There is an element $1 \in R$ such that $1a = a = a1$ for all $a \in R$.

- Associativity of Multiplication: For all $a, b, c \in R$ we have $(ab)c = a(bc)$.

- Distributive Laws: For all $a, b, c \in R$ we have $a(b+c) = ab + ac$ and $(a + b)c = ac + bc$.

Again, note that the multiplication in $R$ need not be commutative. $R$ is an abelian group under addition, but multiplicative inverses need not exist. (An element $u$ of a ring $R$ is called a *unit* of $R$ if there is an element $v \in R$ such that $uv = 1 = vu$.) Also, it's important to be aware that sometimes authors don't insist that a multiplicative identity exists, but we will always say it does. Exercise A.4 below shows that the additive and multiplicative identities are unique; this is what enables us to call them "0" and "1" without ambiguity. Similarly, Exercise A.5 below shows that both the additive inverse and the multiplicative inverse (if it exists) of $a$ are unique, so we denote these inverses by $-a$ and $a^{-1}$ respectively.

Some familiar examples of rings are: $\mathbb{Z}$ (the integers), $\mathbb{Z}/n\mathbb{Z}$ (the integers modulo $n$), $\mathbb{Q}$ (the rationals), $\mathbb{Q}[x]$ (polynomials with rational coefficients), $M_n(\mathbb{Q})$ ($n \times n$ matrices with entries in $\mathbb{Q}$). Note that $M_n(\mathbb{Q})$ is an example where multiplication is not commutative.

**Exercise A.4.** Let $R$ be a ring.

**a)** Suppose that $a$ and $b$ are elements of $R$ such that $a + x = x$ and $b + x = x$ for every $x \in R$. Show that $a = b$.

**b)** Suppose that $c$ and $d$ are elements of $R$ such that $cx = x$ and $dx = x$ for every $x \in R$. Show that $c = d$.

**Exercise A.5.** Let $R$ be a ring and let $a \in R$.

**a)** Suppose that for some $b, c \in R$ we have $a + b = 0 = b + a$ and $a + c = 0 = c + a$. Show that $b = c$.

**b)** Let $a \in R$. Suppose that for some $b, c \in R$, we have $ab = 1 = ba$ and $ac = 1 = ca$. Show that $b = c$.

**Exercise A.6.** Let $i = \sqrt{-1}$ and set $\mathbb{Q}[i] = \{a + bi \mid a, b \in \mathbb{Q}\}$. Show that $\mathbb{Q}[i]$ is a ring under normal addition and multiplication of complex numbers. What is the "0"? What is the "1"? Is this ring commutative? What are the units of this ring?

**Definition A.7.** A *field* is a ring which satisfies two additional properties:

- Commutativity of Multiplication: For all $a, b \in R$, $ab = ba$.
- Existence of Multiplicative Inverses: For all $a \in R \setminus \{0\}$ there is a $b \in R \setminus \{0\}$ such that $ab = 1 = ba$.

Some familiar examples of fields are: $\mathbb{Q}$, $\mathbb{R}$ (the reals), $\mathbb{C}$ (the complex numbers), $\mathbb{Z}/p\mathbb{Z}$ (the integers modulo $p$, where $p$ is prime), $\mathbb{Q}(x)$ (quotients of polynomials with rational coefficients). There are also the finite fields $\mathbb{F}_q$ where $q$ is a power of a prime; we'll look at these more in Appendix B.

**Exercise A.8.** Show that $\mathbb{Z}/p\mathbb{Z}$ is a field if $p$ is prime. Find $2^{-1}$ as an element of $\mathbb{Z}/5\mathbb{Z}$.

We will be working with rings of the form $k[x]$, where $k$ is a field, quite a bit. One important fact about these polynomial rings is that the Division Algorithm holds: If $a(x), b(x) \in k[x]$ with $b(x) \neq 0$, then there are unique $q(x), r(x) \in k[x]$ such that $a(x) = b(x)q(x) + r(x)$, where either $r(x) = 0$, or the degree of the polynomial $r(x)$ is strictly smaller than the degree of the polynomial $b(x)$.

**Exercise A.9.** Let $k = \mathbb{Z}/5\mathbb{Z}$, and set $a(x) = 3x^4 + x^3 + 2x^2 + 1 \in k[x]$, $b(x) = x^2 + 4x + 2 \in k[x]$. Find $q(x), r(x) \in k[x]$ such that $a(x) = b(x)q(x) + r(x)$.

**Definition A.10.** An *ideal* in a ring $R$ is a nonempty subset $I \subseteq R$ which satisfies the following properties:

- Containment of additive identity: $0 \in I$
- Closure under addition: For all $a, b \in I$, $a + b \in I$.
- Containment of additive inverses: For all $a \in I$, $-a \in I$.
- Absorption: If $a \in I$ and $r \in R$ then $ar \in I$ and $ra \in I$.

Note that since $I \subseteq R$ is assumed to be nonempty, the first three conditions above could be replaced by the following single condition:

- Subgroup under addition: For all $a, b \in I$, $a - b \in I$.

It should be mentioned that what we have defined here is actually what is called a two-sided ideal. Left ideals have only half the absorption property: If $a \in I$ and $r \in R$ then $ar \in I$. Right ideals have the other half. If $R$ is commutative, then there's no difference. For us, just defining two-sided ideals will suffice because we will henceforth assume that

*all rings we work with are commutative.*

An ideal $I$ of a (commutative) ring $R$ is called *principal* if there is some $a \in I$ such that $I = \{ar \mid r \in R\}$. In this case we write $I = \langle a \rangle$ or $I = aR$.

Two examples of principal ideals are: the even integers (as an ideal of the integers) and the set of all polynomials $f(x) \in \mathbb{Q}[x]$ satisfying $f(1) = 0$ (this is $(x - 1)\mathbb{Q}[x]$). An example of an ideal which is not principal is $\langle x, y \rangle := \{xf(x,y) + yg(x,y) \mid f, g \in \mathbb{Q}[x,y]\} \subseteq \mathbb{Q}[x,y]$.

**Exercise A.11.** Let $I$ be an ideal of the ring $R$. Show that $I = R$ if and only if some unit of $R$ is in $I$.

**Exercise A.12.** Let $k$ be a field. What are the ideals of $k$?

**Exercise A.13.** Let $k$ be a field. Prove that every ideal of the ring $k[x]$ is principal. Hint: Given an ideal $I$ of $k[x]$, pick $f \in I$ of smallest possible degree and then use the division algorithm.

If $R$ is a ring with operations $+$ and $\cdot$ and $I$ is an ideal of $R$, we can define a new ring $R/I$ called the *factor ring of $R$ modulo $I$*.

To do this, we must say what the set $R/I$ is, and we must give two operations on that set which satisfy all the required properties.

First, we must define cosets. Let $r \in R$. The *coset* of $I$ in $R$ corresponding to $r$ is $r + I = \{r + i \mid i \in I\}$. Now, as a set, we define $R/I$ to be the set of all cosets of $I$ in $R$:

$$R/I := \{r + I \mid r \in R\}$$

**Exercise A.14.** Show that for $r, s \in R$, either $r + I = s + I$ or $(r + I) \cap (s + I) = \emptyset$.

We'll (temporarily) denote the addition on $R/I$ by $\oplus$ and the multiplication by $\odot$ to avoid confusion. Then we define

$$(r + I) \oplus (s + I) = (r + s) + I$$

and

$$(r + I) \odot (s + I) = (rs) + I.$$

The facts that these operations make sense and that they turn $R/I$ into a ring require proof. The proof is tedious but not difficult, so we'll skip most of it. However, you should do the following exercise:

**Exercise A.15.** Show that $\oplus$ and $\odot$ are well-defined. That is, if $a + I = b + I$ and $c + I = d + I$, show that $(a + c) + I = (b + d) + I$ and $ac + I = bd + I$.

Exercise A.15 shows that the operations $\oplus$ and $\odot$ make sense. The following exercise shows that the ring $R/I$ inherits its ideal structure from the ring $R$.

**Exercise A.16.** Let $R$ be a ring and $I$ an ideal of $R$. Show that the ideals of $R/I$ are in one-to-one correspondence with the ideals of $R$ which contain $I$. In particular, show that every ideal of $R/I$ is of the form $J/I$ for some ideal $J$ of $R$ which contains $I$.

One example of a factor ring we'll be looking at is

$$R_n := k[x]/\langle x^n - 1 \rangle$$

where $k$ is a field.

**Exercise A.17.** Prove that elements of $R_n$ are in one-to-one correspondence with polynomials over $k$ of degree at most $n - 1$. Hint: Use the Division Algorithm.

Because of Exercise A.17, we can think of the elements of $R_n$ as actually being polynomials over $k$, as long as we always replace $x^n$ with 1 when doing computations.

**Exercise A.18.** Take $k = \mathbb{Z}/5\mathbb{Z}$ and compute the following in $R_4$ (using the correspondence of Exercise A.17):

a) $(1 + 3x + 5x^3) + (3 + 4x^2 + 2x^3)$

b) $(1 + 3x + 5x^3)(3 + 4x^2 + 2x^3)$

**Exercise A.19.** Let $k$ be any field, $n$ a positive integer, and let $a_0, \ldots, a_{n-1} \in k$. Compute $x(a_0 + a_1x + \cdots + a_{n-1}x^{n-1})$ in $R_n$.

## A.3. Vector Spaces

**Definition A.20.** Let $k$ be a field. A vector space $V$ over $k$ is an abelian group which admits a scalar multiplication by elements of $k$. If we let $+$ denote the group operation and $\cdot$ (or concatenation) denote the scalar multiplication, then the following properties must be satisfied for any $v, w \in V$ and any $\alpha, \beta \in k$:

- $\alpha(v + w) = \alpha v + \alpha w$

- $(\alpha\beta)v = \alpha(\beta v)$

- $(\alpha + \beta)v = \alpha v + \beta v$

- $1_k \cdot v = v$, where $1_k$ is the multiplicative identity of $k$

Elements of $V$ are called *vectors*. Let $V$ be a vector space over $k$ and let $S$ be a subset of $V$. We say $S$ is *linearly independent* if whenever $\alpha_1, \ldots, \alpha_n \in k$ and $v_1, \ldots, v_n \in S$ satisfy $\alpha_1 v_1 + \ldots \alpha_n v_n = 0$, it must be true that $\alpha_1 = \cdots = \alpha_n = 0$. We say $S$ *spans* $V$ if for any $w \in V$ there exist $\alpha_1, \ldots, \alpha_n \in k$ and $v_1, \ldots, v_n \in S$ such that $\alpha_1 v_1 + \ldots \alpha_n v_n = w$. We say $S$ is a *basis* for $V$ if $S$ is linearly independent and spans $V$. In this case, the number of elements of $S$ is called the *dimension* of $V$. In general, there are several linearly independent subsets $S$ which span the vector space $V$, but they all have the same number of elements. In other words, the dimension of $V$ is independent of the choice of basis.

## A.4. Homomorphisms and Isomorphisms

**Definition A.21.** Let $A$ and $B$ be groups, rings, or vector spaces. A *homomorphism* from $A$ to $B$ is a function $\phi : A \to B$ which preserves the operations in $A$ and $B$. In particular,

- If $A$ and $B$ are groups, then for all $x, y \in A$, we have $\phi(xy) = \phi(x)\phi(y)$.
- If $A$ and $B$ are rings, for all $x, y \in A$, we have $\phi(xy) = \phi(x)\phi(y)$ and $\phi(x + y) = \phi(x) + \phi(y)$.
- If $A$ and $B$ are vector spaces over the field $k$, then for all $x, y \in A$ and for all $\alpha \in k$, we have $\phi(x+y) = \phi(x)+\phi(y)$ and $\phi(\alpha x) = \alpha\phi(x)$. (In this case, $\phi$ is often called a *linear transformation* rather than a homomorphism.)

A homomorphism is called an *isomorphism* if it is one-to-one and onto. If there is an isomorphism from $A$ to $B$, we write $A \cong B$ and say that $A$ and $B$ are *isomorphic*. If $\phi : A \to A$ is an isomorphism, we call $\phi$ an *automorphism* of $A$.

Notice that in each equation in the above definition, the operations on the left-hand-side of the equations are occurring in $A$ while the operations on the right are occurring in $B$.

**Definition A.22.** Let $A$ and $B$ be groups, rings, or vector spaces, and let $\phi : A \to B$ be a homomorphism. The *kernel* of $\phi$ is defined to be all the elements of $A$ which get sent to the appropriate identity of $B$. In particular,

- If $A$ and $B$ are groups, then $\ker \phi := \{a \in A \,|\, \phi(a) = e_B\}$.
- If $A$ and $B$ are rings, then $\ker \phi := \{a \in A \,|\, \phi(a) = 0_B\}$.
- If $A$ and $B$ are vector spaces, then $\ker \phi := \{a \in A \,|\, \phi(a) = 0_B\}$.

**Exercise A.23.** Let $A$ and $B$ be groups, rings, or vector spaces, and let $\phi : A \to B$ be a homomorphism.

**a)** Show that $\ker \phi$ is a normal subgroup (if $A$ and $B$ are groups), ideal (if $A$ and $B$ are rings), or vector subspace (if $A$ and $B$ are vector spaces) of $A$.

**b)** Show that $\phi$ is one-to-one if and only if $\ker \phi = \{e_A\}$ (if $A$ and $B$ are groups), $\{0_A\}$ (if $A$ and $B$ are rings), or $\{0_A\}$ (if $A$ and $B$ are vector spaces).

We will need the following theorem:

**Theorem A.24.** (First Isomorphism Theorem) *Let $A$ and $B$ be groups, rings, or vector spaces and let $\phi : A \to B$ be a homomorphism. Then*

$$A/\ker \phi \cong \phi(A).$$

# Appendix B

# Finite Fields

In Exercise A.8, you showed that $\mathbb{Z}/p\mathbb{Z}$ is a field for each prime $p$. Therefore, since there are infinitely many primes, there are infinitely many finite fields. When we think of $\mathbb{Z}/p\mathbb{Z}$ as a field, we will write $\mathbb{F}_p$ rather than $\mathbb{Z}/p\mathbb{Z}$. Fields of the form $\mathbb{F}_p$ are called *prime fields* of characteristic $p$ (see Definition B.1 below). In practice, the most common alphabet for an error-correcting code is $\mathbb{F}_2$, the field with 2 elements. Codes over this alphabet are commonly called *binary*. However, finite fields which are not prime fields are important in coding theory as well. For example, one often uses *extension fields* of $\mathbb{F}_2$ (fields which contain $\mathbb{F}_2$ as a subfield) as a tool in the construction of binary codes. Further, for many theoretical results, finite fields of characteristic other than 2 are needed. The purpose of this appendix is to develop some of the theory of finite fields.

## B.1. Background and Terminology

In this section, we set up some of the needed background and terminology in order to study finite fields. Each definition is followed by an exercise or two.

**Definition B.1.** Let $k$ be a field. The *characteristic* of $k$ is the least positive integer $n$ such that $nx = 0$ for all $x \in k$. If no such $n$ exists, we say that $k$ has characteristic 0.

For example, $\mathbb{Q}$, $\mathbb{R}$, and $\mathbb{C}$ all have characteristic 0, while $\mathbb{F}_p = \mathbb{Z}/p\mathbb{Z}$ has characteristic $p$.

**Exercise B.2.** Explain why every finite field has nonzero characteristic.

**Exercise B.3.** Let $k$ be a field of characteristic $p \neq 0$. Show that $p$ is prime and that $k$ contains $\mathbb{F}_p$ as a subfield.

A *proper ideal* $I$ of a ring $R$ (i.e., an ideal $I$ of $R$ with $I \neq R$) is called a *maximal ideal* if for every ideal $J$ with $I \subseteq J \subseteq R$, either $I = J$ or $J = R$. (In other words $I$ is maximal if it's proper and not contained in any other proper ideal.)

**Exercise B.4.** Show that $I$ is a maximal ideal of $R$ if and only if $R/I$ is a field. (Hint: Exercise A.16)

Let $k$ be a field and let $f(x) \in k[x]$ be a polynomial. We say $f(x)$ is *irreducible* if $f(x) \notin k$ and if whenever $f(x) = g(x)h(x)$ for some $g(x), h(x) \in k[x]$, either $g(x) \in k$ or $h(x) \in k$. (In other words, $f(x)$ is irreducible in $k[x]$ if it's not constant and if it can't be written as the product of two non-constant polynomials in $k[x]$.)

**Exercise B.5.** Let $k$ be a field and $f(x) \in k[x]$. Show that the ideal $\langle f(x) \rangle \subset k[x]$ is maximal if and only if $f(x)$ is irreducible.

## B.2. Classification of Finite Fields

Let $k$ be a field and let $f(x) \in k[x]$ be an irreducible polynomial of degree $d$. As in Exercise A.17, we may think of elements of $k[x]/\langle f(x) \rangle$ as polynomials of degree at most $d - 1$. Now, however, these polynomials will form a field by Exercises B.4 and B.5 above. To avoid confusion, we'll write $\alpha$ for the element of the field $k[x]/\langle f(x) \rangle$ which corresponds to $x$.

**Exercise B.6.** Let $g(x) = x^3 + x + 1 \in \mathbb{F}_2[x]$.

    **a)** Show that $g(x)$ is irreducible in $\mathbb{F}_2[x]$. Conclude that $\mathbb{F} := \mathbb{F}_2[x]/\langle g(x) \rangle$ is a field.

    **b)** How many elements does $\mathbb{F}$ have? List them. Make an addition table and a multiplication table.

**Exercise B.7.** Let $h(x) = x^3 + x^2 + 1 \in \mathbb{F}_2[x]$.

**a)** Show that $h(x)$ is irreducible in $\mathbb{F}_2[x]$. Conclude that $\mathbb{F}' := \mathbb{F}_2[x]/\langle h(x)\rangle$ is a field.

**b)** How many elements does $\mathbb{F}'$ have? List them. Make an addition table and a multiplication table.

**c)** By matching up elements of the addition and multiplication table, show that $\mathbb{F}'$ is isomorphic to the field $\mathbb{F}$ of Exercise B.6 above.

In general, there is the following theorem about finite fields:

**Theorem B.8.** *Let $m$ be a positive integer. Then there is a field with exactly $m$ elements if and only if $m = p^n$ for some prime $p$ and some positive integer $n$. Further, up to isomorphism, there is only one field with exactly $p^n$ elements, and it is of the form $\mathbb{F}_p[x]/\langle f(x)\rangle$ for some irreducible polynomial $f(x) \in \mathbb{F}_p[x]$ of degree $n$. In particular, if $f(x)$ and $g(x)$ are both irreducible polynomials in $\mathbb{F}_p[x]$ of degree $n$, then $\mathbb{F}_p[x]/\langle f(x)\rangle$ and $\mathbb{F}_p[x]/\langle g(x)\rangle$ are isomorphic fields.*

We also have the following theorem, which is useful in proving Theorem B.8 and is important in its own right as well.

**Theorem B.9.** *Let $\mathbb{F}$ be a finite field with $p^n$ elements. Then $\mathbb{F}^\times := \mathbb{F} \setminus \{0\}$ is a cyclic group of order $p^n - 1$.*

An element $\alpha \in \mathbb{F}$ is called *primitive* if $\mathbb{F}^\times = \langle \alpha \rangle$. Theorem B.9 shows that every finite field has at least one primitive element.

Before we can prove Theorem B.9, we need a few facts which are the content of the next exercise.

**Exercise B.10.** Let $k$ be a field and let $g(x) \in k[x]$.

**a)** Suppose $g(r) = 0$ for some $r \in k$. Show that $g(x) = (x-r)f(x)$ for some $f(x) \in k[x]$.

**b)** Show that $g(x)$ has at most $\deg(g)$ roots.

**Proof of Theorem B.9.** First notice that since $\mathbb{F}$ is a field, every nonzero element of $\mathbb{F}$ is a unit and so $\mathbb{F}^\times$ is indeed an abelian group of order $p^n - 1$. Thus, we only need to show that it is cyclic.

By the Fundamental Theorem of Finite Abelian Groups (Theorem A.2), we can write $\mathbb{F}^\times \cong C_{r_1} \oplus \cdots \oplus C_{r_t}$, where $C_r$ is a cyclic group of order $r$, $r_{i+1}$ divides $r_i$ for each $i$, and $r_1 \ldots r_t = p^n - 1$. For any $\beta \in \mathbb{F}^\times$, we have $\beta^{r_1} = 1$, so the polynomial $x^{r_1} - 1$ has at least $p^n - 1$ zeros in $\mathbb{F}$. By Exercise B.10, this shows that $p^n - 1 \leq r_1$. But $\mathbb{F}^\times$ has a subgroup $C_{r_1}$ of order $r_1$, so $p^n - 1 = |\mathbb{F}^\times| \geq r_1$. Thus $p^n - 1 = r_1$, so $\mathbb{F}^\times \cong C_{r_1}$ is cyclic. $\qquad\square$

The usual proof of Theorem B.8 involves Galois Theory, or at least the theory of splitting fields. (One shows that a finite field $\mathbb{F}$ with $p^n$ elements is the splitting field of the polynomial $x^{p^n} - x$.) However, a proof that doesn't require this background is outlined in the optional exercises at the end of this appendix. The basic idea is as follows: First, use a counting argument to show that for every positive integer $n$ there is at least one irreducible polynomial of degree $n$ in $\mathbb{F}_p[x]$. This shows that fields with $p^n$ elements do exist. (This part is elementary but long and hence not included in the exercises, but can be found in [**CLO2**].) Next, if $\mathbb{F}$ is any finite field, we see by Exercise B.3 above that $\mathbb{F}$ contains some prime field $\mathbb{F}_p$ as a subfield. From there, it's not hard to see that $\mathbb{F}$ is a vector space over $\mathbb{F}_p$, which shows that $\mathbb{F}$ has $p^n$ elements for some positive integer $n$. That gives the first statement of the theorem. The rest follows from Theorem B.9.

Because of Theorem B.8, if $p$ is a prime and $n$ is a positive integer, then there is a unique (up to isomorphism) field with $p^n$ elements. Thus we may unambiguously denote this field by $\mathbb{F}_{p^n}$. We know that $\mathbb{F}_p \subseteq \mathbb{F}_{p^n}$ from Exercise B.3. It is also not difficult to show that $\mathbb{F}_{p^m} \subset \mathbb{F}_{p^n}$ if and only if $m$ divides $n$. So for example, $\mathbb{F}_4 \subset \mathbb{F}_{16}$, but $\mathbb{F}_8 \not\subset \mathbb{F}_{16}$. In particular, if $q$ is any prime power and $n \geq 1$, then $\mathbb{F}_q \subset \mathbb{F}_{q^n}$.

We will have occasion to use the *trace map* and the *Frobenius automorphism*, both of which we define below.

**Definition B.11.** Let $q$ be any prime power and let $n \geq 1$. Then the *Frobenius automorphism* is the map $\sigma_{q,n} : \mathbb{F}_{q^n} \to \mathbb{F}_{q^n}$ defined by $\sigma_{q,n}(\alpha) = \alpha^q$ for any $\alpha \in \mathbb{F}_{q^n}$. If $q = p^r$ where $p$ is prime and $r \geq 2$, the map $\sigma_{q,n}$ is often called the *relative Frobenius*, whereas $\sigma_{p,n}$ is often called the *absolute Frobenius*.

**Exercise B.12.** Show that $\sigma_{q,n}$ is one-to-one and onto.

**Exercise B.13.** Show that $\sigma_{q,n}$ is a homomorphism. (Thus, $\sigma_{q,n}$ is an automorphism of $\mathbb{F}_{q^n}$.)

**Exercise B.14.** Show that $\sigma_{q,n}(\alpha) = \alpha$ if and only if $\alpha \in \mathbb{F}_q$.

We will write $\sigma_{q,n}^j$ for the map obtained by composing $\sigma_{q,n}$ with itself $j$ times. For example, $\sigma_{q,n}^2(\alpha) = \sigma_{q,n}(\sigma_{q,n}(\alpha))$.

**Exercise B.15.** Show that for any $\alpha \in \mathbb{F}_{q^n}$, we have $\sigma_{q,n}^n(\alpha) = \alpha$.

**Definition B.16.** Let $q$ be any prime power and let $n \geq q$. The *trace* of an element $\alpha \in \mathbb{F}_{q^n}$ is defined to be $\mathrm{tr}_q(\alpha) = \alpha + \sigma_{q,n}(\alpha) + \cdots + \sigma_{q,n}^{n-1}(\alpha)$. If $q = p^r$ with $r \geq 2$, the map $\mathrm{tr}_q$ is called the *relative trace* while $\mathrm{tr}_p$ is called the *absolute trace*.

**Exercise B.17.** Show that $\sigma_{q,n}(\mathrm{tr}_q(\alpha)) = \mathrm{tr}_q(\alpha)$. Conclude that for any $\alpha \in \mathbb{F}_{q^n}$, $\mathrm{tr}_q(\alpha) \in \mathbb{F}_q$.

## B.3. Optional Exercises

In this section, we outline a proof of Theorem B.8.

**Exercise B.18.** Let $\mathbb{F}$ be a finite field of characteristic $p$. By Exercise B.3 above, we know that $\mathbb{F}_p \subset \mathbb{F}$. Show that $\mathbb{F}$ is a vector space over $\mathbb{F}_p$. Conclude that since $\mathbb{F}$ has only finitely many elements, $\mathbb{F}$ must have finite dimension $n$ over $\mathbb{F}_p$, so that the cardinality of $\mathbb{F}$ is $p^n$.

**Exercise B.19.** Let $\mathbb{F}$ be a finite field. We know from Exercise B.18 that the number of elements in $\mathbb{F}$ is some prime power $p^n$. Let $\alpha$ be a primitive element of $\mathbb{F}$. Define a ring homomorphism $\phi : \mathbb{F}_p[x] \to \mathbb{F}$ by $\phi(x) = \alpha$.

  **a)** Explain why $\phi$ is onto.

  **b)** Show that there is some irreducible polynomial $g(x) \in \mathbb{F}_p[x]$ such that $\ker \phi = \langle g(x) \rangle$.

  **c)** Conclude that $\mathbb{F} \cong \mathbb{F}_p[x]/\langle g(x) \rangle$.

**Exercise B.20.** Let $\mathbb{F}$, $\mathbb{F}'$ be two fields with $p^n$ elements. We wish to show that $\mathbb{F} \cong \mathbb{F}'$. (We did this in the case $p^n = 8$ in Exercises B.6 and B.7 above.)

a) Let $\alpha \in \mathbb{F}$ be primitive and write $\mathbb{F} \cong \mathbb{F}_p[x]/\langle g(x)\rangle$ as in Exercise B.19 above. Show that $g(x)$ divides $(x^{p^n} - x)$ in $\mathbb{F}_p[x]$.

b) Show that $x^{p^n} - x$ factors completely in $\mathbb{F}'[x]$. In other words, show that
$$x^{p^n} - x = \prod_{\beta \in \mathbb{F}'} (x - \beta).$$

c) Deduce that there is some $\gamma \in \mathbb{F}'$ satisfying $g(\gamma) = 0$.

d) Deduce that $\mathbb{F}' \cong \mathbb{F}_p[x]/\langle g(x)\rangle$, hence that $\mathbb{F} \cong \mathbb{F}'$.

# Appendix C

# Projects

We have discussed only the very basics of classical coding theory – just enough to motivate algebraic geometry codes and see why they are important. Below are six important topics in coding theory which we omitted.

## C.1. Dual Codes and Parity Check Matrices

Let $C$ be a linear code. As we saw, $C$ has a generator matrix. There is also such a thing as a *parity check matrix* for $C$, and this matrix turns out to be a generator matrix for the *dual code* $C^\perp$. Find out the definitions of the parity check matrix and the dual codes. Also, there's a relationship described by the *MacWilliams Identities* (named after Florence Jesse MacWilliams, who discovered them) between the weights of codewords of $C$ and the weights of codewords of $C^\perp$. Find out what you can on this as well. Note: The people doing Projects C.3 and C.6 below may want to consult with you.

## C.2. BCH Codes

An important class of cyclic codes is the BCH codes. Find out what you can about these codes, including their construction and their parameters. It turns out that the Reed-Solomon codes (and maybe the Generalized Reed-Solomon codes, too) can be thought of as BCH codes. How?

## C.3. Hamming Codes

The Hamming codes are another important family of codes. They are both cyclic (which we discussed in class) and *perfect* (you'll need to find out what this means). Decoding (figuring out which codeword was sent if errors occur in transmission) with Hamming codes is very easy because of the especially simple form of the parity check matrix (Project C.1) of these codes. Be sure to report on the parameters of these codes. Note: The people doing Project C.4 below may want to consult with you.

## C.4. Golay Codes

The Golay codes are famous for many reasons. Find out what you can about this family of codes. The original paper in which they were defined is incredibly short! Find it. Those of you who have had finite group theory will be interested to know that the automorphism group of the binary Golay code of length 24, dimension 12, and minimum distance 8 is $M_{24}$, a finite simple group (called a Mathieu group) of order 244823040. Like the Hamming codes (Project C.3), the Golay codes are perfect.

## C.5. MDS Codes

Recall that MDS codes are codes with parameters which meet the Singleton bound. The Reed-Solomon codes are MDS codes. Are there other examples? The Main Conjecture on MDS Codes was mentioned briefly in Chapter 2.1. What is it? What sort of progress has been made towards proving it? What other ideas are involved?

## C.6. Nonlinear Codes

We've focused almost entirely on linear codes, but there are several families of nonlinear codes out there with very good parameters. Some examples are the Kerdock codes and the Preparata codes. Learn about these families, and in particular about the Nordstrom Robinson code, which is a member of both families. There's an important relationship between the Kerdock codes and the Preparata codes involving the MacWilliams Identities (see Project C.1) – what is it? A 1994 paper by Hammons and others showed that several well-known families of nonlinear binary codes are actually linear if viewed in a certain way. Find out what you can about this.

# Bibliography

[CLO1]   D. Cox, J. Little, and D. O'Shea, *Ideals, Varieties, and Algorithms. An Introduction to Computational Algebraic Geometry and Commutative Algebra*, Second Edition. Springer-Verlag, New York. 1997

[CLO2]   D. Cox, J. Little, and D. O'Shea, *Using Algebraic Geometry*, Springer-Verlag, New York, 1998.

[F]   W. Fulton, *Algebraic Curves. An Introduction to Algebraic Geometry*, W.A. Benjamin, inc. New York, New York, 1969.

[Ga]   J. A. Gallian, *Contemporary Abstract Algebra*, Fourth Edition. Houghton Mifflin, Boston, 1998. Goppa

[Go]   V. D. Goppa, "Codes associated with divisors", *Probl. Peredachi Inf.*, **13**, (1977), pp. 33-39. English translation in *Probl. Inf. Transm.*, **13** (1977) pp. 22-27.

[H]   R. Hartshorne, *Algebraic Geometry*, Springer-Verlag, New York, 1977.

[I]   Y. Ihara, "Some remarks on the number of rational points of algebraic curves over finite fields", *J. Fac. Sci. Univ. Tokyo Sect. IA Math.* **28** (1981), pp. 721-724.

[LG]   J. H. Van Lint and Gerard Van Der Geer, *Introduction to Coding Theory and Algebraic Geometry*, Birkhauser-Verlag, Boston, 1988.

[L]   J. H. Van Lint, *Introduction to Coding Theory*, Third Edition. Springer-Verlag, New York, 1999.

[MS]   F. J. MacWilliams and N. J. A. Sloane, *The Theory of Error-Correcting Codes*, Elsevier Science Publishers B.V. New York, 1997.

[NZM]  I. Niven, H. S. Zuckerman, and H. L. Montgomery, *An Introduction to the Theory of Numbers*, Fifth Edition. John Wiley & Sons, Inc., New York, 1991.

[R]  M. Reid, *Undergraduate Algebraic Geometry*, Cambridge University Press, Cambridge, 1988

[ST]  J. H. Silverman and J. Tate, *Rational Points on Elliptic Curves*, Springer-Verlag, New York, 1992.

[S]  H. Stichtenoth, *Algebraic Function Fields and Codes*, Springer-Verlag, New York, 1993.

[TVZ]  M. A. Tsfasman, S. G. Vladut, and Th. Zink, "Modular curves, Shimura curves, and Goppa Codes, better than the Varshamov-Gilbert bound", *Math. Nachrichten*, **109** (1982), pp. 21-28.

[TV]  M. A. Tsfasman and S. G. Vladut, *Algebraic-Geometric Codes*, Kluwer Academic Publishers, Boston, 1991.

[V]  L. R. Vermani, *Elements of Algebraic Coding Theory*, Chapman & Hall, New York, 1996.

[VD]  S. G. Vladut and V. G. Drinfeld, " The number of points of an algebraic curve", *Funktsional. Anal. i Prilozhen.* **17** (1983), pp. 68-69. English translation in *Functional Anal. Appl.* **17** (1983), pp. 53-54.}

[W]  R. J. Walker, *Algebraic Curves*, Dover Publications inc. New York, 1950.